How to Start & Manage a Plumbing Service Business

A Practical Way to Start Your Own Business

by Jerre G. Lewis and Leslie D. Renn

How to Start & Manage
A Plumbing Service Business

Lewis & Renn Associates, Inc.
Business & Professional Publishing
10315 Harmony Drive
Interlochen, Michigan 49643
(231) 275-7287

Leslie D. Renn
President

Jerre G. Lewis
Secretary-Treasurer

ISBN # 978-1-57916-175-0
Library of Congress Catalog Card Number
99-094172

TABLE OF CONTENTS

Chapter 1

Introduction

Selecting the right Plumbing Service business opportunity requires careful, thorough evaluations of yourself. Owning your own business is as much a part of the American dream as owning a home, and for you, this urge represents one of life's most exciting challenges. This book is for those men and women who someday may go into business for themselves and for those who are already in business for themselves but wish to strengthen their entrepreneurial and managerial skills.

Entrepreneurs come in all shapes and sizes, personalities, and lifestyles. They are usually highly motivated, hard-working individuals who receive satisfaction from taking risks. Your business should interest you, not just be an income generator. Analyze your personal style. Do you like working with people? Are you a self starter, goal oriented, persistent, a risk taker, willing to work hard and long hours?

If you have been honest in evaluating yourself, you will now select the right type of business. Before you can determine which of the multitude of businesses is right for you to start, you must evaluate the businesses you want to start by asking these questions. Is the business area growing? How does the economy affect it? Who dominates its market? Once you have considered a business that satisfies your needs and interest you must prepare a formal business plan by following the outline given in this book.

Small businesses constitute a dynamic and critical sector of the U.S. economy. Every year in the United States more than 600,000 new businesses are launched by independent men and women eager to make their own decisions, express their own ideas, and be their own bosses. But running your own business is not as easy as it may seem. There can be problems with the inventory, or getting the right goods delivered on time. Yet, managing one's own business can be a personally and financially rewarding experience for an individual strong enough to meet the test. A person with stamina, maturity, and creativity, one who is willing to make sacrifices, may find making a go of a struggling enterprise an exhilarating challenge with many compensations.

Small business owners are a dedicated group of people who work hard and whose hours on the job usually exceed the nine-to-five routine. The owner's commitment is the key to many successful small businesses; an entrepreneur is able to communicate ideas, lead, plan, be patient, and work well with people.

Managing a business requires more than the possession of technical knowledge. Because most small businesses are started by technical people, such as engineers and salesmen, their managerial acumen is often less developed than their technical skills. The need to plan for management is common to every type of and size of business, and there are certain steps that must be taken. Although some of them are very elementary — such as applying for a city business permit — the most important are often complex and difficult and require the advice of specialists: accountants, attorneys, insurance brokers, and/or bankers. For almost any business though, the first step will be to translate the entrepreneur's basic idea into a concrete plan for action.

To gauge your level of entrepreneurial spirit, the following quiz was created. Please answer each question honestly and then total the columns.

ENTREPRENEURIAL QUIZ

	YES	NO	SOMETIMES
1. I am a self-starter. Nobody has to tell me how to get going.	____	____	_____
2. I am capable of getting along with just about everybody.	____	____	_____
3. I have no trouble getting people to follow my lead.	____	____	_____
4. I like to be in charge of things and see them through.	____	____	_____
5. I always plan ahead before beginning a project. I am usually the one who gets everyone organized.	____	____	_____
6. I have a lot of stamina. I can keep going as long as necessary.	____	____	_____
7. I have no trouble making decisions and can make up my mind in a hurry.	____	____	_____
8. I say exactly what I mean. People can trust me.	____	____	_____
9. Once I make my mind up to do something, nothing can stop me.	____	____	_____
10. I am in excellent health and have a lot of energy.	____	____	_____

	YES	NO	SOMETIMES

11. I have experience or
    technical knowledge in
    the business I intend to
    start.

    _____   _____   _____

12. I feel comfortable taking
    risks if it is something
    I really believe in.

    _____   _____   _____

13. I have good communication
    skills.

    _____   _____   _____

14. I am flexible in my dealings
    with people and situations.

    _____   _____   _____

15. I consider myself creative
    and resourceful.

    _____   _____   _____

16. I can analyze a situation
    and take steps to correct
    problems.

    _____   _____   _____

17. I think I am capable of
    maintaining a good
    working relationship
    with employees.

    _____   _____   _____

18. I am not a dictator.
    I am willing to listen to
    employees, customers
    and suppliers.

    _____   _____   _____

19. I am not rigid in my policies.
    I am willing to adjust to
    meet the needs of employees,
    customers, and suppliers.

    _____   _____   _____

20. More than anything else,
    I want to run my own
    business.

    _____   _____   _____

Total of Column #1   _____

Total of Column #2   _____

Total of Column #3   _____

If the total of Column #1 is the highest, then you will probably be very successful in running your own business.

If the total of Column #2 is the highest, you may find that running a business is more than you can handle.

If the total of Column #3 is the highest, you should consider taking on a partner who is strong in your weak areas.

NOTE: This quiz was adapted from the Small Business Administration publication *Checklist for Going Into Business.*

Notes _____

Chapter 2

Planning the Business

The Dream of self-employment can be fulfilled. You don't need to finance the opening of an elaborate office or facility to start your own one-person corporation either. You can start your own Plumbing Service business.

Anyone preparing to run an Plumbing Service business needs to learn a great deal to assure the best possible chance for success.

GETTING STARTED

The following is a list of what you need to accomplish to insure that your Plumbing Service endeavor will head in the right direction.

1. Define your educational background and work experience.

2. Survey all the basic types of Plumbing Service businesses.

3. Define what products or services your Plumbing Service business will be marketing.

4. Define who will be using your products/services.

5. Define why they will be purchasing your products/services.

6. List all competitors in your Plumbing Service marketing area.

ZONING REGISTRATIONS

Plumbing Service businesses are subject to many laws and regulations enforced by state, county, township governmental units. Most jurisdictions now have codes, a zoning board, and an appeal board which regulate businesses. Areas often are zoned residential, commercial or industrial.

You must become familiar with these regulations. If you are doing business in violation of these regulations, you could be issued a cease and desist order or fined.

Certain kinds of goods cannot be produced in the home, though these restrictions vary somewhat from state-to-state. Most states outlaw home production of fireworks, drugs, poisons, explosives, sanitary/medical products and some toys.

Many localities have registration requirements for new businesses. You will need to obtain a work certificate or license from the state.

TAX REQUIREMENTS

Application for Employer Identification Number, Form SS-4. This registers you with the Internal Revenue Service as a business. If you have employees, you should ask for Circular E along with your ID number. Circular E explains federal income and social security tax withholding requirements.

Employer's Annual Unemployment Tax Return, Form 940. This is only if you have employees. It's used to report and pay the Federal Unemployment Compensation Tax.

Employee's Withholding Allowance Certificate, W-4. Every employee must complete the W-4 so the proper amount of income tax can be withheld from the employee's pay. If the employee claims more than 15 allowances or a complete withholding exemption while having a salary of more than $200 a week, a copy of the W-4 must go to the IRS.

Employer's Wage and Tax Statement, W-2. Used to report to the IRS the total taxes withheld and total compensation paid to each employee per year.

Reconciliation/Transmittal of Income and Tax Statements, W-3. Used to total all information from the W-2. Sent to the Social Security Administration.

The IRS puts on monthly workshops on understanding and using these forms. Call your local IRS office for further information.

States also have various tax form requirements including: an unemployment tax form, a certificate of registration application, a sales and use tax return, an employer's quarterly contribution and payroll report, an income tax withholding registration form, an income tax withholding form, and others. Some forms apply only to employers who have employees. Your local IRS office and state Office of Taxation can provide you with listings of forms you will need to start your business. The following table outlines Federal tax form requirements.

Every small business begins with an idea — a product to be manufactured or sold, a service to be performed.

Whatever the business or its degree of complexity, the owner needs a business plan in order to transform a vision into a working operation.

This business plan should describe in writing and in figures the proposed Plumbing Service business and its products, services, or manufacturing processes. It should also include an analysis of the market, a marketing strategy, an organizational plan, and measurable financial objectives.

WHAT SHOULD A BUSINESS PLAN COVER?

It should be a thorough and objective analysis of both personal abilities and business requirements for a particular product or service. It should define strategies for such functions as marketing and production, organization and legal aspects, accounting and finance. A business plan should answer such questions as:

What do I want and what am I capable of doing?
What are the most workable ways of achieving my goals?
What can I expect in the future?

There is no single best way to begin. What follows is simply a guide and can be changed to suit individual needs.

1. Define Long-term goals.
2. State short-term.
3. Set marketing strategies to meet goals and objectives.
4. Analyze available resources.
5. Assemble financial data.
6. Review plan.

Please refer to Figure 2.1 for a complete business plan outline.

The business operator with a realistic plan has the best chance for success.

Figure 2.1

BUSINESS PLAN FOR SMALL BUSINESSES

   I.   Type of Business

  II.   Location

 III.   Target Market

 IV.   Planning Process

   V.   Organizational Structure

 VI.   Staffing Procedures

VII.   Market Strategy

 IX.   Financial Planning

   X.   Budgeted Balance Sheet

 XI.   Budgeted Income Statement

XII.   Budgeted Cash Flow Statement

XIII.   Break-Even Chart

Notes

Chapter 3

Marketing Strategies
for an Plumbing Service Business

As a potential Plumbing Service business owner, it is important to learn all you can about marketing. You will need to know how to identify your market and how to market your product or service.

As a business person who looks for a profit from the sale of goods, you recognize that without people who want to buy, there is no demand for the things you want to sell. Thus, it is important that, in addition to knowing about the functions of marketing, you also study the activities that will influence the consumer. When you satisfy the specific needs and wants of the customer, then he or she may be willing to pay you a price that will include a profit for you — and to make a profit is one of the reasons you have become an Plumbing Service business owner. Although there are many activities connected with marketing, most of them can be classified in these categories: buy, finance, transport, standardize, store, insure, advertise and sell.

Target Market Analysis

Before you can create a successful marketing campaign, it's necessary to determine your target market (toward whom to direct your energies). The whole concept of target marketing can seem very scary at first. On the surface, targeting appears to be limiting the scope of the pool of potential customers. Many people fear that by defining a market, they will lose business. They are concerned that they will choose the wrong market. Or that other practitioners will take just anybody and therefore some of their business.

You must keep in mind that the purpose of defining your target market is to make your life easier and increase the productivity of your promotional endeavors. Many opportunities exist in this world and it's impossible to pursue them all or be everything to everyone. You need to know where to focus your energy and money when it comes to promotion and advertising.

The two most common means of market analysis are demographics and psychographics, which describe a person in terms of objective data and personality attributes.

Demographics are statistics such as:
- age
- gender
- income level
- geographic location
- occupation
- education level

Psychographics are lifestyle factors including:
- special interest activities
- philosophical beliefs
- social factors
- cultural involvements

The more you know about your potential customers, the easier it is to develop an appropriate position statement and design an effective marketing campaign. The actual number of target markets you have depends mainly upon the size of your practice and the scope of your knowledge.

Your Target Market Profile

In order to clarify your target market(s) you need to delineate the demographic and psychographic factors and then identify the characteristics your customers have in common.

Describe your current customers and those who are most likely your future customers:

What is the age range and average age of your customers?

What is the percentage of males?

What is the percentage of females?

What is the average educational level of your customers?

Where do your customers live?

What are the occupations of your customers?

Where do your customers work?

What is the average annual income level of your customers?

Of what special interest groups are your customers members?

What is the primary reason your customers use your services?

Defining Your Target Market(s)

Write a descriptive statement for each of your target markets (refer to your "Target Market Profile"). Include a brief overview of the services you are providing to that group and a detailed analysis of the characteristics of the specific clientele.

Target Market 1:

Target Market 2:

Target Market 3:

Plumbing Service Business Marketing

The foundation for creating a thriving customer base.

A. Overview

This section is about clarifying your beliefs and attitudes toward your profession and determining the image you wish to portray.

1. Describe the "character" that you want for your business.
   Depict the image you want to convey:

2. State your philosophy in regard to your business:

3. Describe your philosophy regarding your practice in business:

B. Customer Profile

This is a descriptive analysis of your current and potential customers — who they are, what their interests are, and where you can find them. Include each of your target markets.

1. Target Market 1:

2. Target Market 2:

3. Target Market 3:

C. Competition's Marketing Assessment

The first phase in planning your promotional campaign is appraising the competition. List each of your major competitors and describe the marketing strategies they utilize. Be certain to include where and how often they advertise.

1. Major Competitor 1:

2. Major Competitor 2:

3. Major Competitor 3:

4. Major Competitor 4:

5. Major Competitor 5:

6. Major Competitor 6:

Plumbing Service Marketing Planning

Outline for Marketing:

I. Produce/Service Concept
    A. Name of produce or service
    B. Descriptive characteristics of product or service
    C. Unit sales
    D. Analysis of market trends

II. Number of Customers in Market Area:
    A. Profile of customers
    B. Average customer expenditure
    C. Total market

III. Your Market Potential:
    A. Total market divided by competition
    B. Total market multiplied by percent who will buy your product

IV. Needs of Customers:
    A. Identification
    B. Pleasure
    C. Social approval
    D. Personal interest
    E. Price

V. Direct Marketing Sources:
    A. Trade magazines
    B. Trade associates
    C. Small Business Administration (SBA)
    D. Government publications
    E. Yellow Pages
    F. Marketing directories

VI. Customer Profile:
    A. Geographical
    B. Gender
    C. Age range
    D. Income brackets
    E. Occupation
    F. Educational level

Chapter 4

Promoting the Plumbing Service Business

When a new business is opened, the owner must be prepared to publicize the business or its chance for success will be slim. Only a few businesses — such as those with a prime location, nationally known name, or a built-in clientele — can succeed without advertising to promote market awareness and stimulate sales.

The first purpose — promoting customer awareness — applies as much to established businesses as to newcomers.

In the Plumbing Service business, you will find it easier to retain old customers than to win new ones. When old customers move away from your area, or when their buying needs change, you need new customers to maintain your sales volume. If you expect your business to gain, you will need additional new customers. New customers are those who move into your area or who have grown into your line of products because now they can afford them or they need them. We see advertising and we hear advertising all around us, and yet that is only a part of it. Through advertising, you call the attention of customers to your products.

As a small business owner, you may advertise your business through your location. People pass by and are attracted to your operation because of what you are selling. To get a better idea of what advertising is, consider some of the following functions of advertising:

1. *To inform:* Letting customers know what you have for sale through brochures, leaflets, newspapers, radio, TV, and etc.

2. *Persuade:* Persuasion is the art of leading individuals to do what you want them to do. There are sales personnel who have persuasive sales presentations, but persuasion in advertising is nonpersonal. The appeal is made through the printed or spoken words or a picture. The influence of an ad on readers occurs as purchasers choose what they want among different products, and different wants. To gain the actions you want — a sale — you must persuade a customer to examine personally what you have for sale.

3. *Reminder:* Advertising performs it's third function when it reminds those who have been persuaded to buy once that the same product will bring satisfaction. The ad will also remind a customer of the characteristics of a product purchased some time ago, and where he or she bought it. Because customers change their loyalty to a place of business, their taste for products, and often their trading area patronage, advertising is necessary to draw new customers and to hold old customers. To generate results from advertising that will be profitable to your business, you will have to produce answers to the what, where and how of advertising.

What to Advertise

The nature of your business will partially answer the question "Shall I advertise goods or services?" What are the outstanding features of your business? Is it unique in any way? Does it have strong points? Do you have something to offer that the competition is not able to duplicate? Answers to these questions will give you a start in deciding what to advertise.

Where to Advertise

Of course, you will want to advertise within your marketing area, however there are a few guidelines to remember:

A. Who are your customers?

B. What is their income range?

C. Why do they buy?

D. How do they buy? Do they pay Cash? Charge?

E. What is the radius of your market area?

How to Advertise:

In determining how to advertise, you will have to consider your dollar allocation for advertising and the media suitable to your particular kind of business. However, it is important to have a balance between the presentation of the product or service being advertised and the application of three basic principles.

1. Gain the attention of the audience.

2. Establish a need.

3. Tell where that need may be filled.

See Figure A for an outline of the different advertising media and Figure B for budget on media goals.

Advertising Media

Media	Market Coverage	Type of Audience
Daily Newspaper	Single community or entire metro area; zoned editions sometimes available	General
Weekly Newspaper	Single community	Residents
Telephone Directory	Geographical area or occupational field served by the directory	Active shoppers for goods or services
Direct mail audience	Controlled by the advertiser	Controlled
Radio audience	Definable market area	Selected
Television audience	Definable market area	Various
Outdoor	Entire metro area	General auto drivers
Magazine	Entire metro area or magazine region	Selected audience

Figure A

Promotion and Advertising Plan — Plumbing Service Business

In designing your promotional plan, it's wise to use a variety of media. You must have specific goals, time lines and budgets for each marketing application

Media	Goal	Timeline	Budget

Notes _____

Chapter 5

Financial Planning for an Plumbing Service Business

Financial planning is the process of analyzing and monitoring the financial performance of your business so you can assess your current position and anticipate future problem areas. The daily, monthly, seasonal, and yearly operation of your business requires attention to the figures that tell you about the firm's financial health.

Maintaining good financial records is a necessary part of doing business.

The increasing number of governmental regulations alone makes it virtually impossible to avoid keeping detailed records. Just as important is to keep them for yourself. The success of your business depends on them. An efficient system of record keeping can help you to:

- make management decisions
- compete in the marketplace
- monitor performance
- keep track of expenses
- eliminate unprofitable merchandise
- protect your assets
- prepare your financial statements

Financial skills should include understanding of the balance sheet, the profit-and-loss statement, cash flow projection, break-even analysis, and source and application of funds. In many businesses, the husband and wife run the business; it is especially important that both of them understand financial management. Most small business owners are not accountants, but they must understand the tool of financial management if they are going to be able to measure the return on their investment. Although good records are essential to good financial planning, they alone are not enough because their full use requires interpretation and analysis. The owner/manager's financial decisions concerning return on invested funds, approaches to banks, securing greater supplier credit, raising additional equity capital and so forth, can be more successful if he takes the time to develop understanding and use of the balance sheet and profit-and-loss statement.

Balance Sheet:

The balance sheet, Figure I, shows the financial condition of a business at the end of business on a specific day. It is called a balance sheet because the total assets balance with, or are equal to, total liabilities plus owner's capital balance. Current assets are those that the owner does not anticipate holding for long. This category includes cash, finished goods in inventory, and accounts receivable. Fixed assets are long-term assets, including plant and equipment. A third possible category is the intangible asset of goodwill. Liabilities are debts owed by the business, including both accounts payable, which are usually short-term, and notes payable, which are usually long-term debts such as mortgage payments. The difference between the value of the assets and the value of the liabilities is the capital. This category includes funds invested by the owner plus accumulated profits, less withdrawals.

The Income Statement:

This statement, Figure II, is also known as a profit-and loss (P&L) statement. It shows how a business has performed over a certain period of time. An income statement specifies sales, costs of sales, gross profit, expenses and net income or loss from operations.

Figure I

Financial Forecast

Opening Balance Sheet - Date

ASSETS

Current Assets

Cash and bank accounts		$
Accounts receivable		$
Inventory		$
Other current assets		$ _____
TOTAL CURRENT ASSETS	(A)	$ _____

Fixed Assets

Property owned		$
Furniture and equipment		$
Business automobile		$
Leasehold improvements		$
Other fixed assets		$ _____
TOTAL FIXED ASSETS	(B)	$ _____
TOTAL ASSETS	(A+B = X)	$ _____

LIABILITIES

Current Liabilities (due within the next 12 months)

Bank loans		$
Other loans		$
Accounts payable		$
Other current liabilities		$ _____
TOTAL CURRENT LIABILITIES	(C)	$ _____

Long-term Liabilities

Mortgages		$
Long-term loans		$
Other long-term liabilities		$ _____
TOTAL LONG-TERM LIABILITIES	(D)	$ _____
TOTAL LIABILITIES	(C+D = Y)	$ _____
NET WORTH	(X-Y = Z)	$ _____
TOTAL NET WORTH AND LIABILITIES	(Y+Z)	$ _____

Figure II

Business Income and Expense Forecast for the Next 12 Months

One year estimate ending _____, 19 _____

Projected Number of Clients

For your services   _____

For your products   _____

TOTAL NUMBER OF CLIENTS   _____

Projected Income

Sessions $ _____

Product sales $ _____

Other $ _____

TOTAL INCOME $ _____

Projected Expenses

Start-up costs $ _____

Monthly expenses (x 12) $ _____

Annual expenses $ _____

TOTAL EXPENSES $ _____

TOTAL OPERATING PROFIT (OR LOSS) $ _____

CAPITAL REQUIRED FOR THE NEXT 12 MONTHS $ _____

Plumbing Service Business

Start-Up Costs Worksheet	
Item	**Estimated Expense**
Open checking account	$
Telephone installation	$
Equipment	$
First & last month's rent, security deposit, etc.	$
Supplies	$
Business cards, stationery, etc.	$
Advertising and promotion package	$
Decorating and remodeling	$
Furniture and fixtures	$
Legal and professional fees	$
Insurance	$
Utility deposits	$
Beginning inventory	$
Installation of fixtures and equipment	$
Licenses and permits	$
Other	$
TOTAL	$

Fixed Annual Expense Worksheet	
Item	**Estimated Expense**
Property insurance	$
Business auto insurance	$
Licenses and permits	$
Liability insurance	$
Disability insurance	$
Professional society membership	$
Fees (legal, accounting, etc.)	$
Taxes	$
Other	$
TOTAL	$

Monthly Business Expense Worksheet		
Expense	**Estimated Monthly Cost**	**X 12**
Rent	$	$
Utilities	$	$
Telephone	$	$
Bank fees	$	$
Supplies	$	$
Stationery and business cards	$	$
Networking club dues	$	$
Education (seminars, books professional journals, etc.)	$	$
Business car (Payments, gas, repairs, etc)	$	$
Advertising and promotion	$	$
Postage	$	$
Entertainment	$	$
Repair, cleaning and maintenance	$	$
Travel	$	$
Business loan payments	$	$
Salary/Draw	$	$
Staff salaries	$	$
Miscellaneous	$	$
Taxes	$	$
Professional fees	$	$
Decorations	$	$
Furniture and fixtures	$	$
Equipment	$	$
Inventory	$	$
Other	$	$
TOTAL MONTHLY	$	$
TOTAL YEARLY		$

	January Estimate	January Actual	February Estimate	February Actual	March Estimate	March Actual
Cash Flow Forecast						
Beginning cash						
Plus monthly income from: Fees						
Sales						
Loans						
Other						
TOTAL CASH AND INCOME						
Expenses:						
Rent						
Utilities						
Telephone						
Bank fees						
Supplies						
Stationery and business cards						
Insurance						
Dues						
Education						
Auto						
Advertising and promotion						
Postage						
Entertainment						

Cash Flow Forecast (Continued)						
	January Estimate	January Actual	February Estimate	February Actual	March Estimate	March Actual
Repair and maintenance						
Travel						
Business loan payments						
Licenses and permits						
Salary/Draw						
Staff salaries						
Taxes						
Professional fees						
Decorations						
Furniture and fixtures						
Equipment						
Inventory						
Other Expenses						
TOTAL EXPENSES						
ENDING CASH (+/-)						

Notes

Chapter 6

Plumbing Service Business Planning

Introduction

Our increasingly service oriented economy offers a widening spectrum of opportunities for customized and personalized small business growth. Though untrained entrepreneurs have traditionally had a high rate of failure, small businesses can be profitable. Success in a small Plumbing Service business is not an accident. It requires both skills in a service or product area and acquisition of management and attitudinal competencies.

The purpose of this publication is to help you take stock of your interests, aptitudes and skills. Many people have good business ideas but not everyone has what it takes to succeed. If you are convinced that a profitable Plumbing Service business is attainable, this publication will provide step-by-step guidance in development of the basic written business plan.

Information Gathering

A helpful tool for use in determining if you are ready to take the risks of an Plumbing Service business operation is the SMA publication entitled *Going Into Business* (MP-12).

It will help you focus on the basic steps in information gathering and business planning.

33

Careful planning is required to research legal and tax issues, proper space utilization and to establish time management discipline. Inadequate or careless attention to development of a detailed business plan can be costly for you and your family in terms of lost time, wasted talent and disappearing dollars.

The Entrepreneurial Personality

A variety of experts have documented research that indicates that successful small business entrepreneurs have some common characteristics. How do you measure up? On this checklist, write a "Y" if you believe the statement describes you; a "N" if it doesn't; and a "U" if you can't decide:

_____ I have a strong desire to be my own boss.

_____ Win lose or draw, I want to be master of my own financial destiny.

_____ I have significant specialized business ability based on both my education and my experience.

_____ I have an ability to conceptualize the whole of a business; not just its individual parts, but how they relate to each other.

_____ I develop an inherent sense of what is "right" for a business and have the courage to pursue it.

_____ One or both of my parents were entrepreneurs; calculate risk-taking runs in the family.

_____ My life is characterized by a willingness and capacity to preserver.

_____ I possess a high level of energy, sustainable over long hours to make the business successful.

While not every successful Plumbing Service business owner starts with a "Y" answer to all of these questions, three or four "N"s and "U"s should be sufficient reason for you to stop and give a second thought to going it alone. Many proprietors who sense entrepreneurial deficiencies seek extra training a support their limitations with help from a skilled team of business advisors such as accountants, bankers and attorneys.

Selecting a Business

A logical first step for the undecided is to list potential areas of personal background, special training, education and job experience, and special interests that could be developed into a business. Review the following list of activities which have proven marketable for others. On a scale of "0" (no interest or strength) to "10" (maximum interest or strength) indicate the potential for you and a total score for each activity.

Time Management

For both the novice and the experienced business person planning a small Plumbing Service enterprise, an early concern requiring self-evaluation is time management.

It is very difficult for some people to make and keep work schedules even in a disciplined office setting. As your own boss the problem can be much greater. To determine how much time you can devote to your business, begin by drafting a weekly task timetable listing all current and potential responsibilities and the blocks of time required for each. When and how can business responsibilities be added without undue physical or mental stress on you or your family? Potential conflicts must be faced and resolved at the outset and as they occur, otherwise your business can become a nightmare. During the first year of operation, continue to chart, post and checkoff tasks on a daily, weekly and monthly basis.

Distractions and excuses for procrastination abound. It is important to keep both a planning and operating log. These tools will help avoid oversights and provide vital information when memory fails.

To improve the quality of work time, consider installation of a telephone line for the business and attaching an answering machine to take messages when you do not wish to be distracted or are away from your business. A business line has the added advantage of allowing you to have a business listing in the phone book and if you wish to buy it, an ad in the classified directory.

Is an Plumbing Service Business Site Allowable?

Now you will want to investigate potential legal and community problems associated with operating the business. You should gather, read and digest specialized information concerning federal, state, county and municipal laws and regulations concerning Plumbing Service business operations.

Check first! Get the facts in writing. Keep a topical file for future reference. Some facts and forms will be needed for your business plan. There may be limitations enforced that can make your planned business impossible or require expensive modifications to your property.

Items to be investigated, recorded and studied are:

TO DO   DONE

_____   _____   county or city zoning code restrictions
_____   _____   necessary permits and licenses for operation
_____   _____   state and local laws and codes regarding zoning
_____   _____   deed or lease restrictions such as covenants and
                                        restrictive conditions of purchase

		parking and customer access; deliveries
_____	_____	parking and customer access; deliveries
_____	_____	sanitation, traffic and noise codes
_____	_____	signs and advertising
_____	_____	state and federal code requirements for space, ventilation, heat and light
_____	_____	limitations on the number and type of workers. If not, check with the local Chamber of Commerce office
_____	_____	reservations that neighbors may have about a business next to or near them

Here are some ways to collect your information. Call or visit the zoning office at county headquarters or city hall. In some localities the city or county Office of Economic Development has print materials available to pinpoint key "code" items affecting a business.

Even in rural areas, the era of unlimited free enterprise is over. Although the decision makers may be in the state capital or in a distant regional office of a federal agency, check before investing in inventory, equipment or marketing programs. If in doubt, call the state office of Industrial Development or the nearest SBA district office. In some states the county agent or home demonstration agent will have helpful information concerning rural or farm business development.

Is the Business Site Insurable?

In addition to community investigations, contact your insurance company or agent. It is almost certain that significant changes will be required in your coverage and limits when you start a business. When you have written a good description of your business, call your agent for help in insuring you properly against new hazards resulting from your business operations such as:

- Fire, theft and casualty damage to inventories and equipment
- business interruption coverage
- fidelity bonds for employees
- liability for customers, vendors and others visiting the business
- workmen's compensation
- group health and life insurance
- product liability coverage if you make or sell a product; workmanship liability for services
- business use of vehicle coverage

Overall Plumbing Service Site Evaluation

After you have gathered as much information as seems practical you may wish to evaluate several different locations. Here's a handy checklist. Using the "0" to "10" scale, grade these vital factors:

Factors to Consider

Factor	Grades 0-10
1. Customer convenience	_____
2. Availability of merchandise or raw materials	_____
3. Nearby competition	_____
4. Transportation availability and rates	_____
5. Quality and quantity of employees available	_____
6. Availability of parking facilities	_____

7. Adequacy of utilities (sewer, water, power, gas) _____

8. Traffic flow _____

9. Tax burden _____

10. Quality of police and fire services _____

11. Environmental factors _____

12. Physical suitability for future expansion _____

13. Provision for future expansion _____

14. Vendor delivery access _____

15. Personal convenience _____

16. Cost of operation _____

17. Other factors including how big you get without moving _____

TOTALS _____

Writing the Business Plan

Now that your research and plan development is nearing completion, it is time to move into action. If you are still in favor of going ahead, it is time to take several specific steps. The key one is to organize your dream scheme into a business plan.

What is it?

- As a business plan it is written by the Plumbing Service business owner with outside help as needed
- It is accurate and concise as a result of careful study
- It explains how the business will function in the marketplace
- It clearly depicts its operational characteristics
- It details how it will be financed
- It outlines how it will be managed
- It is the management and financial "blueprint" for start-up and profitable operation
- It serves as a prospectus for potential investors and lenders

Why create it?

- The process of putting the business plan together, including the thought that you put in before writing it, forces you to take an objective, critical, unemotional look at your entire business proposal
- The finished written plan is an operational tool which, when properly used, will help you manage your business and work toward its success
- The completed business plan is a means for communicating your ideas to others and provides the basis for financing your business

Who should write it?

- The Plumbing Service owner to the extend possible
- Seek assistance in weak areas, such as:
  - accounting
  - insurance
  - capital requirements
  - operational forecasting
  - tax and legal requirements

When should a business plan be used?

- To make crucial start-up decisions
- To reassure lenders or backers
- To measure operations progress
- To test planning assumptions
- As a basis for adjusting forecasts
- To anticipate ongoing capital and cash requirements
- As the benchmark for good operations management

Proposed Outline for Plumbing Service Business Plan

This outline is suggested for a small proprietorship or family business. Shape it to fit *your* unique needs. For more complex manufacturing or franchise operations see the Resource section for other options.

Part I - Business Organization

Cover page:

A. Business name:
    Street address:
    Mailing address:
    Telephone number:
    Owner(s) name(s):

Inside pages:

B. Business form:
    (proprietorship, partnership, corporation)

    If incorporated (state incorporation)

    Include copies of key subsidiary documents in an appendix.

Remember even partnerships require written agreements of terms and conditions to avoid later conflicts and to establish legal entities and equities. Corporations require charters, articles of incorporation and bylaws.

Part II - Business Purpose and Function

In this section, write an accurate yet, concise description of the business. Describe the business you plan to start in narrative form.

What is the principal activity? Be specific. Give product or service description(s):

- retail sales?

- manufacturing?

- service?

- other?

How will it be started?

- a new start up

- the expansion of an existing business

- purchase of a going business

- a franchise operation

- actual or projected start up date

Why will it succeed? Promote your idea!

- how and why this business will be successful

- what is unique about your business

- what is its market "niche"

What is your experience in this business? If you have a current resume of your career, include it in an appendix and reference it here. Otherwise write a narrative here and include a resume in the finished product. If you lack specific experience, detail how you plan to gain it, such as training, apprenticeship or working with partners who have experience.

The Marketing Plan

The marketing plan is the core of your business rationale. To develop a consistent sales growth an Plumbing Service business person much become knowledgeable about the market. To demonstrate your understanding, this section of the Plumbing Service business plan should seek to concisely answer several basic questions:

Who is your market?

- Describe the profile of your typical customer
  Age?
  Male, female, both?
  How many in family?
  Annual family income?
  Location?
  Buying patterns?
  Reason to buy from you?

Other?

- Biographically describe your trading area (i.e., county, state, national)

- Economically describe your trading area: (single family, average earnings, number of children)

How large is the market?

- Total units or dollars?

- Growing _____ Steadily _____ Decreasing _____

- If growing, annual growth rate. _____

Who is your competition?

No small business operates in a vacuum. Get to know and respect the competition. Target your marketing plans. Identify direct competitors (both in terms of geography and product lines), and those who are similar or marginally comparative. Begin by listing names, addresses and products or service. Detail briefly but concisely the following information concerning each of your competitors:

- Who are the nearest ones?

- How are their businesses similar or competitive to yours?

- Do you have a unique "niche"? Describe it.

- How will your service or product be better or more saleable than your competitors?

- Are their businesses growing? Stable? Declining? Why?

- What can be learned from observing their operations or talking to their present or former clients?

- Will you have competitive advantages or disadvantages? Be honest!

What percent of the market will you penetrate?

1. estimate the market in total units or dollars

2. estimate your planned volume

3. amount your volume will add to total market

4. subtract 3 from 2

Item 4 represents the amount of your planned volume that must be taken away from the competition.

What pricing and sales terms are you planning?

The primary consideration in pricing a product or service is the value that it represents to the customer. If, on the previous checklist of features, your product is truly ahead of the field, you can command a premium price. On the other hand, if it is a "me too" product, you may have to "buy" a share of the market to get your foothold and then try to move price up later. This is always risky and difficult. One rule will always hold: ultimately, the market will set the price. If your selling price does not exceed your costs and expenses by the margin necessary to keep your business healthy, you will fail. Know your competitors pricing policies. Send a friend to comparison shop. Is there discounting? Special sales? Price leaders? Make some "blind" phone calls. Detail your pricing policy.

What is your sales plan?

Describe how you will sell, distribute or service what you sell. Be specific. Below are outlined some common practices:

Direct Sales - by telephone or in person. The tremendous growth of individual sales representatives who sell by party bookings, door to door, and through distribution of call back promotional campaigns suggests that careful research is required to be profitable.

Mail Order - Specialized markets for leisure time or unique products have grown as more two income families find less time to shop. Be aware of recent mail order legislation and regulation.

Franchising -

a. You may decide to either buy into someone else's franchise as a franchisee, or

b. Create your own franchise operation that sells rights to specific territories or product lines to others. Each will require further legal, financial and marketing research.

Management Plan

Who will do what?

Be sure to include four basic sets of information:

1. State a personal history of principals and related work, hobby or volunteer experience (include formal resumes in Appendix)

2. List and describe specific duties and responsibilities of each

3. List benefits and other forms of compensation for each

4. Identify other professional resources available to the business: Example: Accountant, lawyer, insurance broker, banker. Describe relationship of each to business: Example "Accountant available on part-time hourly basis, as needed, initial agreement calls for services not to exceed x hours per month at $xx.xx per hour."

To make this section graphically clear, start with a simple organizational chart that lists specific tasks and shows, *who* (type of person is more important than an individual name other than for principals) will do *what* indicate by arrows, work flow and lines of responsibility and/or communications. Consider the following examples:

or like this?

As the service business grows, its organization chart could look like this:

The Financial Plan

Clearly the most critical section of your business plan document is the financial plan. In formulating this part of the planning document, you will establish vital schedules that will guide the financial health of your business through the troubled waters of the first year and beyond.

Before going into the details of building the financial plan, it is important to realize that some basic knowledge of accounting is essential to the productive management of your business. If you are like most business owners, you probably have a deep and abiding interest in the product or services that you sell or intend to sell. You like to do what you do, and it is even more fulfilling that you are making money doing it. There is nothing wrong with that. Your conviction that what you are doing or making is worthwhile is vitally important to success. Nonetheless, the income of a coach who takes the greatest pride in producing a winning team will largely depend on someone keeping score of the wins and losses.

The business owner is no different. Your product or service may improve the condition of mankind for generations to come, but, unless you have access to an unlimited bankroll, you will fail if you don't make a profit. If you don't know what's going on in your business, you are not in a very good position to assure its profitability.

Most Plumbing Service businesses will use the "cash" method of accounting with a system of record keeping that may be little more than a carefully annotated checkbook in which is recorded all receipts and all expenditures, backed up by a few forms of original entry (invoices, receipts, cash tickets). For a Sole Partnership, the business form assumed by this Management Aid, the very minimum of recorded information is that required to accurately complete the Federal Internal Revenue Service Form 1040, Schedule C. Other business types (partnerships, joint ventures, corporations) have similar requirements but use different tax forms.

If your business is, or will be, larger than just a small supplement to family income, you will need something more sophisticated. Stationery stores can provide you with several packaged small business account systems complete with simple journals and ledgers and detailed instructions in understandable language.

Should you feel that your accounting knowledge is so rudimentary that you will need professional assistance to establish your accounting system, the classified section of your telephone directory can lead you to a number of small business services that offer a complete range of accounting services. You can buy as much as you need, from a simple "pegboard" system all the way to computerized accounting, tax return service and monthly profitability consultation. Rates are reasonable for the services rendered and an investigative consultation will usually be free. Look under the heading, "Business Consultants," and make some calls.

Let's start by looking at the makeup of the financial plan for the business.

The Financial plan includes the following:

1. Financial Planning Assumptions - these are short statements of the conditions under which you plan to operate.

- Market health
- Date of start-up
- Sales build-up ($)
- Gross profit margin
- Equipment, furniture and fixtures required
- Payroll and other key expenses that will impact the financial plan

2. Operations Plan - Profit and Loss Projection - this is prepared for the first year's Budget. Appendix A-11.

3. Source of Funds Schedule - this shows the source(s) of your funds to capitalize the business and how they will be distributed among your fixed assets and working capital.

4. Pro Forma Balance Sheet - "Pro forma" refers to the fact that the balance sheet is before the fact, not actual. This form displays Assets, Liabilities and Equity of the business. This will indicate how much Investment will be required by the business and how much of it will be used as Working Capital in its operation.

5. Cash Flow Projection - this will forecast the flow of cash into and out of your business through the year. It helps you plan for staged purchasing, high volume months and slow periods.

Creating the Profit and Loss Projection.

Appendix A-11. Create a wide sheet of analysis paper with a three inch wide column at the extreme left and thirteen narrow columns across the page. Write at the top of the first page the planned name of your business. On the second line of the heading, write "Profit and Loss Projection." On the third line, write "First Year."

Then, note the headings on Appendix A-11 and copy them onto your 12-column sheet, copy the headings from the similar area on Exhibit A. Then follow the example set by Appendix A-11 and list all of the other components of your income, cost and expense structure. You may add or delete specific loans of expense to suit your business plan. Guard against consolidating too many types of expenses under one account lest you lose control of the components. At the same time, don't try to break down expenses so discretely that accounting becomes a nuisance instead of a management tool. Once again, Exhibit A provides ample detail for most businesses.

Now, in the small column just to the left of the first monthly column, you will want to note which of the items in the left-hand column are to be estimated on a monthly (M) or yearly (Y) basis. Items such as Sales, Cost of Sales and Variable expenses will be estimated monthly based on planned volume and seasonal or other estimated fluctuations. Fixed Expenses can usually be estimated on a yearly basis and divided by twelve to arrive at even monthly values. The "M" and "Y" designations will be used later to distinguish between variable and fixed expense.

Depreciation allowances for Fixed Assets such as production equipment, office furniture and machines, vehicles, etc. will be calculated from the Source of Funds Schedule.

Appendix A-11 describes line by line how the values on the Profit and Loss Projection are developed. Use this as your guide.

Source of Funds Schedule

To create this schedule, you will need to create a list of all the Assets that you intend to use in your business, how much investment each will require and the source of funds to capitalize them. A sample of such a list is shown below:

Asset	Cost	Source of Funds
Cash	$2,500	Personal savings
Accounts Receivable	3,000	From profits
Inventory	2,000	Vendor credit
Pickup truck	5,000	Currently owned
Packaging machine	10,000	Installment purchase
Office desk and chair	300	Currently owned
Calculator	75	Personal cash
Electric typewriter*	500	Personal savings

* A note about office equipment, test use or rent two or more brands that appear to meet your needs and select the one with which you feel most comfortable. Don't be afraid to ask others who have had to make this decision for advice. Compatibility of your system with those of potential typesetting services or printers should be of high considerations. If you are not quite sure, consider renting or leasing the equipment until you are. Service contracts on such complex electronic gear are usually a good insurance policy.

Before you leave your Source of Funds Schedule, indicate the number of months (years x 12) of useful life for depreciable fixed assets. (An example, the pickup truck, the packaging machine and the furniture and office equipment would be depreciable.) Generally, any individual item of equipment, furniture, fixtures, vehicles, etc., costing over $100 should be depreciated. For more information on allowances for depreciation, you can get free publications and assistance from your local Internal Revenue Service office. Divided the cost of each fixed asset item by the number or months over which it will be depreciated. You will need this data to enter as monthly depreciation on your Profit and Loss Projection. All of the data on the Source of Funds Schedule will be needed to create the Balance Sheet.

Creating the Pro Forma Balance Sheet

Appendix A-13. This is the Balance Sheet Form. There are a number of variations of this form and you may find it prudent to ask your banker for the form that the bank uses for small business. It will make it easier for them to evaluate the health of your business. Use this to get started and transfer the data to your preferred form later. Accompanying Appendix A-12 which describes line by line how to develop the Balance Sheet.

Even though you may plan to stage the purchase of some assets through the year, for the purpose of this pro forma Balance Sheet, assume that all assets will be provided at the start-up.

Cash Flow Projection

An important subsidiary schedule to your financial plan is a monthly Cash Flow Projection. Prudent business management practice is to keep no more cash in the business than is needed to operate it and to protect it from catastrophe. In most small businesses, the problem is rarely one of having too much cash. A Cash Flow Projection is made to advise management of the amount of cash that is going to be absorbed by the operation of the business and compares it against the amount that will be available.

SBA has created an excellent form for this purpose and it is shown as Appendix B. Your projection should be prepared on 13-column analysis paper to allow for a twelve-month projection. Appendix B represents a line by line description and explanation of the components of the Cash Flow Projection which provides a step-by-step method of preparation.

Resources

U.S. Small Business Administration
Office of Business Development

Business Development Publication
MP15

Plumbing Service
Business Associations for the Entrepreneur

American Supply Association (ASA)
222 Merchandise Mart, Ste. 1360
Chicago, IL 60654
Peter Schwartz, Exec. VP
PH: (312) 464-0090   FX: (312) 464-0091
Founded: 1970   Members: 1,200

Cnetral Wholesalers Association (CSA)
P.O. Box 310
Caledonia, OH 43314-0310
Dan L. Schosser, Exec. VP
PH: (419) 845-2023   FX: (419) 845-2026
Founded: 1974   Members: 111

Wholesale Distributors Association (WDA)
10875 Plano Rd., Ste 115
Dallas, TX 75238
Cyrus Farver, Exec. VP
PH: (214) 349-7100   FX: (214) 349-7946
Founded: 1929   Members: 140

Notes _____

Chapter 7

Managing The Business

Delegating work, responsibility, and authority is difficult in a small business because it means letting others make decisions which involved spending the owner/manager's money. At a minimum, he should delegate enough authority to get the work done, to allow assistants to take initiative, and to keep the operation moving in his absence. Coaching those who carry responsibility and authority in self-improvement is essential and emphasis in allowing competent assistants to perform in their own style rather than insisting that things be done exactly as the owner/manager would personally do them is important. "Let others take care of the details" is the meaning of delegating work and responsibility. In theory, the same principles for getting work done through other people apply whether you have 25 employees and one top assistant or 150 to 200 employees and several keymen yet, putting the principles into practice is often difficult.

Delegation is perhaps the hardest job owner/managers have to learn. Some never do. They insist on handling many details and work themselves into early graves. Others pay lip service to the idea but actually run a one-man shop. They give their assistants many responsibilities but little or no authority. Authority is the fuel that makes the machine go when you delegate word and responsibility. If an owner/manager is to run a successful company, he must delegate authority properly. How much authority is proper depends on your situation. At a minimum, you should delegate enough authority: (1) to get the work done, (2) to allow keymen to take initiative, (3) to keep things going in your absence.

The person who fills a key management spot in the organization must either be a manager or be capable of becoming one. A manager's chief job is to plan, direct, and coordinate the work of others. He should possess the three "I's" — Initiative, Interest, and Imagination. The manager of a department must have enough self-drive to start and keep things moving. Personality traits must be considered. A keyman should be strong-willed enough to overcome opposition when necessary.

When you manage through others, it is essential that you keep control. You do it by holding a subordinate responsible for his actions and checking the results of those actions. In controlling your assistants, try to strike a balance. You should not get into a keyman's operations so closely that you are "in his hair" nor should you be so far removed that you lose control of things.

You need feedback to keep yourself informed. Reports provide a way to get the right kind of feedback at the right time. This can be daily, weekly, or monthly depending on how soon you need the information. Each department head can report his progress, or lack of it, in the unit of production that is appropriate for his activity; for example, items packed in the shipping room, sales per territory, hours of work per employee.

For the owner/manager, delegation does not end with good control. It involves coaching as well, because management ability is not required automatically. You have to teach it. Just as important, you have to keep your managers informed just as you would be if you were doing their jobs.

Part of your job is to see that they get the facts they need for making their decisions. You should be certain that you convey your thinking when you coach your assistants. Sometimes words can be inconsistent with thoughts. Ask questions to make sure that the listener understands your meaning. In other words, delegation can only be effective when you have good communications.

Sometimes an owner/manager finds himself involved in many operational details even though he does everything that is necessary for delegation of responsibility. In spite of defining authority, delegation, keeping control, and coaching, he is still burdened with detailed work. Usually, he had failed to do one vital thing. He has refused to stand back and let the wheels turn.

If the owner/manager is to make delegation work, he must allow his subordinates freedom to do things their way. He and the company are in trouble if he tries to measure his assistants by whether they do a particular task exactly as he would do it. They should be judged by their results — not their methods. No two persons react exactly the same in every situation. Be prepared to see some action taken differently from the way in which you would do it even though your policies are well defined. Of course, if an assistant strays too far from policy, you need to bring him back in line. You cannot afford second-guessing.

You should also keep in mind that when an owner/manager second-guesses his assistants, he risks destroying their self-confidence. If the assistant does not run his department to your satisfaction and if his shortcomings cannot be overcome, then replace him. But when results prove his effectiveness, it is good practice to avoid picking at each move he makes.

Chapter 8

Business Resource Information

Books

Steps To: Small Business Start-up,
by Linda Pinson and Jerry Jinnett (Kaplan Publishing, 2006).

Blue's Clues for Success: The 8 Secrets Behind a Phenomenal Business,
by Diane Tracy (Dearborn, 2001).

Entrepreneur Magazine's Start Your Own Business, 3rd. ed.,
by Rieva Lesonsky (Entrepreneur Press, 2004).

MBA in a Day: What You Would Learn at the Top-Tier Business Schools,
by Steven Stralser (New York: John Wiley & Sons, 2004).

Own Your Own Corporation: Why the Rich Own Their Own Companies and Everyone Else Works for them,
by Garrett Sutton, Robert T. Kiyosaki, and Ann Blackman (Warner Books, 2001).

Portratis of Success: 9 Keys to Sustaining Value in Any Business,
by James Olan Hutcheson (Dearborn, 2002).

Small Time Operator: How to Start Your Own Business, Keep Your Books, Pay Your Taxes, and Stay Out of Trouble, (Small Time Operator, 27th Edition)
by Bernard B. Kamoroff, (Bell Springs Publishing, 2005).

Successful Business Planning in 30 Days: A Step-by-Step Guide for Writing a Business Plan and Starting Your Own Business,
by Peter J. Patsula (Patsul Media, 2000).

Straight Talk About Starting and Growing Your Business,
by Sanjyot P. Dunung (McGraw Hill, 2006).

Associations and Organizations

U.S. Department of Commerce
14th Street and Constitution Avenue NW
Room 5055
Washington, DC 20210
Phone: 202-482-5061
Web site: *rvwm.mbda.gov*

U.S. Department of Labor
200 Constitution Avenue NW
Washington, DC 20210
Web site: *www.dol.gov*

Federal Trade Commission
600 Pennsylvania Avenue NW
Washington, DC 20580
General information: 202-326-2222
Anti-trust and competition issues: 202-326-3300
Web site: *www.ftc.gov*

U.S. Small Business Administration (SBA)
403 3rd Street SW
Washington, DC 20416
Phone: 202-205-7701
Web site: *www.sba.gov*

SBA Regional Offices
- Region 1, Boston: 617-565-8415
- Region 2, New York: 212-264-1450
- Region 3, King of Prussia, PA: 215-962-3700
- Region 4, Atlanta: 404-347-995
- Region 5, Chicago: 310-353-5000
- Region 6, Ft. Worth, TX: 817-885-6581
- Region 7, Kansas City, MO: 816-374-6380
- Region 8, Denver: 303-844-0500
- Region 9, San Francisco: 415-744-2118
- Region 10, Seattle: 206-553-7310

Internal Revenue Service
Washington, DC 20224
Phone: 800429-1040
Web site: *www.irs.ustres.gov*

The IRS has an expansive Web site where you can find a great deal of tax help and a state-by-state guide for locating state tax information. There are also numerous tax publications (all numbered) including:

- Tax Guide for Small Business, Publication #334
- Self-Employment Tax, Publication #533
- Business Expenses, Publication #535

For tax forms go to *www.irs.ustres.gov/forms*

International Franchise Association
1350 New York Avenue NW
Suite 900
Washington, DC 20005-4709
Phone: 202-628-8000

American Association of Franchises and Dealers
P.O. Box 81887
San Diego, CA 92138-1887
Phone: 800-733-9858
Web site: *www.aafd.org*

Associations and Organizations

**National Association of Women
 Business Owners**
1411 K Street NW
Suite 1300
Washington, DC 20005
Phone: 202-347-8686
Fax: 202-347-4130
Information service line: 800-556-2926
Web site: *www.nawbo.org*

The National Association for the Self-Employed
1023 15 Street NW
Suite 1200
Washington, DC 20005-2600
Phone: 202-466-2100
Web site: *www.nase.com*
The NASE works to help the self-employed
make their businesses successful and provides
numerous benefits and services. It was formed
over twenty years ago by small business owners.

**Occupational Safety and Health Administra-
tion (OSHA)**
200 Constitution Avenue NW
Washington, DC 20210
Web site: *www.osha-slc.gov*

Institute For Occupational Safety and Health
Phone: 800-35-NIOSH or 513-533-8328
Web site: *www.cdc.gov/niosh*

Dun & Bradstreet
Austin, Texas 78731
Phone: 800-234-3867
Web site: *www.dnb.com*
For over 160 years, D&B has been providing
companies with information and assistance in
making key business decisions.

**American Entrepreneurs for
 Economic Growth**
1655 North Fort Myer Drive
Suite 850
Arlington, VA 22209
Phone: 703-524-3743
Web site: *www.aeeg.org*

**National Association of
 Home-Based Businesses**
10451 Mill Run Circle
Suite 400
Owings Mills, MD 21117
Phone: 410-363-3698
Web site: *www.usahomebusiness.com*

U.S. Census Bureau
Washington DC 20233
Phone: 301-457-4608
Web site: *www.census.gov*

U.S. Patent and Trademark Office
General Information Services Division
Crystal Plaza 3, Room 2CO2
Washington, DC 20231
Phone: 800-786-9199 or 703-308-4357
Web site: *www.uspto.gov*

U.S. Securities & Exchange Commission
450 Fifth Street NW
Washington, DC 20549
Office of Investor Education
 and Assistance: 202-942-7040
Web site: *www.sec.gov*

Associations and Organizations

American Association of
   Home Based Businesses
Fax: 301-963-7042
P.O. Box 10023
Rockville, MD 20849
Website: *www.aahbb.org*

American Small Businesses Association
800-942-2722
8773 IL Route 75E
Rock City, IL 61070

Home Business Institute
561-865-0865
P.O. Box 480215
Delray Beach, FL 33448
Website: *www.hbiweb.com*

Marketing Research Association
860-257-4008
1344 Silas Deane Highway, Suite 306,
Rocky Hill, CT 06067
Website: *www.mra-net.org*

National Association of the
   Self-Employed (NASE)
800-252-NASE (800-232-6273)
P.O. Box 612067
DFW Airport
Dallas, TX 75261-2067
Website: *www.nase.org*

Magazines

Entrepreneur Magazine, Business Start-Ups Magazine, and **Entrepreneur's Home Office**
Entrepreneur Media, Inc.
2392 Morse Avenue
Irvine, CA 92614
Phone: 714-261-2325
Web site: *www.entrepreneurmag.com*

Forbes
60 Fifth Avenue
New York, NY 10011
Phone: 212-620-2200
Web site: *www.forbes.com*

Inc. Magazine
38 Commercial Wharf
Boston, MA 02110
Phone: 617-248-8000 or 800-2340999
Web site: *www.inc.com*

My Business Magazine
Hammock Publishing, Inc.
3322 West End Avenue
Suite 700
Nashville, TN 37203
Phone: 615-385-9745

Consumer Goods Manufacturer
Edgell Communications
10 West Hanover Avenue
Suite 107
Randolph, NJ 07869

Minority Business Entrepreneur
3528 Torrance Boulevard
Suite 101
Torrance, CA 90503
Phone: 310-540-9398
Web site: *www.mbemag.com*

Workforce ACC Communications
245 Fischer Avenue
Suite B-2
Costa Mesa, CA 92626
Phone: 714-751-4106
Web site: *www.workforceonline.com*

Websites

www.allbusiness.com
A comprehensive site with resources for small and medium sized businesses.

www.bizweb.com
A guide to some 47,000 companies.

www.bplan.com
Numerous sample business plans for various industries.

www.bspage.com
The Business Start page includes a short course on starting a business, tips, and reviews of top business books.

www.business.gov
The U.S. Business Advisor is a one-stop shop for working with the many government agencies that impact upon business.

www.businessfinance. com
A major online source for finding potential investors.

www.businessnation.com
Business news, a library, discussions, opportunities, and resources.

www.businesstown.com
Information and articles from starting to selling your business.

www.catalogconsultancy.com
Information and guidance for catalog and direct mail businesses.

www.chamber-of-commerce.com
Links to local chamber of commerce Web sites, and e-mail addresses.

www.financenet.com
Sponsored by the US Chief Financial Officers Council, FinanceNet has a wealth of information and resources available specializing in public financial management.

www.globalbizdirectory.com
Massive director of retail, agricultural, mining, and numerous other business-related organizations and associations. Includes a state-by-state and international listing database.

www.gomez.com
Gomez offers business new and detailed report cards and consumer responses on e-commerce Web sites in various sectors.

www.homebusiness.com
Detailed information and business solutions for the home base business.

www.hoovers.com
Provides detailed business and company information, industry report links, professional help, business news, and more.

www.ideacafe.com
A good place for news, tips, expert advice ideas, and schmoozing with other small business owners.

www.inc.com
A wealth of articles and advice about starting and growing your business from the folks at Inc. Magazine.

www.marketingsource.com/associations
Find any association in any industry at this valuable resource site.

www.morebusiness.com
Articles, tips, sample business and marketing plans, legal forms contracts, a newsletter, and more offered for entrepreneurs.

www.nasbic.org
The National Association of Small Business Investment Companies promotes growth in the business sector through numerous programs.

Library Resources

Almanac of Business and Industrial Financial Ratios
(Prentice-Hall). Provides ratios and industry norms in actual dollar figures derived from IRS data. Each industry includes performance indicators such as total assets, cost of operations, wages, and profit margins.

American Wholesaler and Distributor Directory
(Gale Research). Provides listings of wholesalers and distributors sorted by product category and state.

Catalog of Catalogs
(Woodbine House). Contains descriptions and contact information for more than 14,000 catalogs, indexed by subject and company name.

Directory of Manufacturers' Sales Agencies
(Manufacturing Agents National Association). Lists manufacturers' sales agencies alphabetically and by state. Also has information on how to select a sales agent.

Encyclopedia of Associations
(Gale Research). Guise to national and international associations; contains contact information and descriptions; indexed by name, key word, and geographic area.

Financial Studies of the Small Business
(Financial Research Associates). Organized by industry; contains financial ratios and indicators for small and microbusinesses.

Lifestyle Market Analyst
(Standard Rate & Data Service). Reference book containing demographic and psychographic statistics for metropolitan statistical areas in the United States.

Small business Profiles
(Gale Research). Contains sources of information related to starting specific types of small businesses. Typical entries include start-up information, trade associations and publications, statistics, and supply sources.

Thomas Food Industry Register.
Directory of food manufacturers and suppliers to the food industry.

Thomas Register of Manufacturing.
Directory of most manufacturing firms; includes company profile and contact information.

The Small Business Administration

The U.S. Small Business Administration was established in 1953 to provide financial, technical, and management assistance to entrepreneurs. Statistics show that most small business failures are due to poor management. For this reason, the SBA places special emphasis on business management training that covers such topics as planning, finance, organization, and marketing. Often, training is held in cooperation with educational institutions, chambers of commerce, and trade associations. Prebusiness workshops are held on a regular basis for prospective business owners. Other training programs are conducted that focus on special needs such as rural development and international trade. One-on-one counseling is provided through the Service Corps of Retired Executives (SCORE) and Small Business Development Centers (SBDC). The SBA strives to match the needs of a specific business with the expertise available.

To access the SBA: Online http://www.sba.gov
                     SBA Answer Desk 800-827-5722

SCORE is a volunteer program that helps small business owners solve their operating problems through free one-on-one counseling and through a well-developed system of low-cost workshops and training sessions. To located a SCORE counseling center in your area or to consult online, access the following site: http://www.score.org
SBDCs are generally located or headquartered in academic institutions and provide individual counseling and practical training for prospective and current business owners. To locate a center near you, log on to http://www.sba.gov/sbdc.

A Concise Guide To Starting Your Own Business

Page A-2

Guide Overview

A concise overview of the complete guide to starting and operating a successful business.

The following topics are presented:

- Business Plan for Small Businesses.
- Getting Started
- Deciding Where To Start The Business
- Business Patronage Statistics
- Site Location
- Site Selection Criteria — Some General Questions.
- Choosing The Proper Method of Organization
- What Is A Corporation?
- Estimating Start-up Costs
- Preparing An Income Statement
- Preparing A Balance Sheet
- Marketing The Business
- Marketing Planning — An Outline for Marketing
- Advertising Media
- Management and Getting The Work Done
- Sample Organization Chart
- Summary of the Business Plan
- Guide Summary
- Reference Materials

Business Plan for Small Businesses

I. Type of Business

II. Location

III. Target Market

IV. Planning Process

V. Organizational Structure

VI. Staffing Procedures

VII. Control

VIII. Market Strategy

IX. Financial Planning

X. Budgeted Balance Sheet

XI. Budgeted Income Statement

XII. Budgeted Cash Flow Statement

XIII. Break-even Chart

Page A-4

Getting Started

Following is a list of what you need to accomplish to insure that your business endeavor will head in the right direction.

1. Define your educational background and work experience

2. Survey all basic types of businesses.

3. Define what type of business matches your experience and educational background.

4. Choose only the business that you would like to own and operate.

5. Define what products or services your business will be marketing.

6. Define who will be using your products/services.

7. Define why they will be purchasing your products/services.

8. List all competitors in your marketing area.

Deciding Where to Start the Business

Will your business fulfill a need in the area you plan to bring your business to? This section provides you with some important information you need to examine before taking your ideas any further:

1. Decide where you want to live.

2. Choose several areas that would match your priorities.

3. Use the list that follows as a guide to see if your location will match the estimated population needed to support your business. The numbers which follow the type of business indicate the typical number of inhabitants per year.

Business Patronage Statistics

Food Stores
Grocery Stores 1,534
Meat and Fish
   (Sea Food) Markets . . . 17,876
Candy, Nut, and
   Confectionery Stores . . 31,409
Retail Bakeries 12,563
Dairy Products Stores . . . 41,587

Eating and Drinking
Restaurant, Lunch Rooms . 1,583
Cafeterias 19,341
Refreshment Places 3,622
Drinking Places 2,414

General Merchandise
Variety Stores 10,373
General Merchandise 9,837

Apparel/Accessories Stores
Women's Ready-To-
   Wear Stores 7,102
Women's Accessory and
   Specialty Stores 25,824
Men's and Boy's Clothing
   and Furnishings 11,832
Family Clothing 16,890
Shoe Stores 9,350

Furniture, Home Furnishings, and Equipment Stores
Furniture Stores 7,210
Floor Covering 29,543
Drapery, Curtains, and
   Upholstery Stores 62,585
House, Appliances 12,485
Radios and TV's 20,346
Record Shops 112,144
Musical Instruments 46,332

Building Materials, Hardware, and Farm Equipment Dealers
Lumber and other Building
   Materials Dealers 8,124
Paint, Glass, and Wallpaper
   Stores 22,454
Hardware Stores 10,206
Farm Equipment Dealers . 14,793

Automotive Dealers
Motor Vehicle Dealers,
   New and Used Cars 6,000
Motor Vehicle Dealers,
   Used Cars only 17,160
Tire, battery, and
   Accessory Dealers 8,800

Boat Dealers 61,500

Household Trailer Dealers . 44,746

Gasoline Service Stations . . . 1,395

Miscellaneous
Antique and Secondhand
   Stores 17,170
Book and Stationery Stores 28,580
Drugstores 4,268
Florists 13,531
Fuel Oil Dealers 25,000
Garden Supply Stores . . . 65,000
Gift, Novelty Shops 26,000
Hobby, Toy, and Game
   Shops 61,000
Jewelry Stores 13,400
Optical Goods Stores 62,800
Sporting Goods Store 27,000

From *Starting and Managing a Small Business of Your Own, 1973;*
Small Business Administration, Washington, DC

Site Location

1. Define your number of inhabitants per store.

2. Locate several sites/locations that will match your inhabitants per stores.

3. Define population and its growth potential.

4. Define local ordinances and zoning regulations that you will need in order to start your type of business.

5. Define your trading area and all competitors in your trading area.

6. Define parking need, for your kind of business.

7. Define special needs, etc., lighting, heating, ventilation.

8. Define rental cost of site/location.

9. Define why customers will come to your site/location.

10. Define the future of your site/location as to population growth.

11. Define your space needs and match with site/location selection.

12. Define the image of your business and make sure it matches your site/location.

Site Selection Criteria — Some General Questions

- Is the site centrally located to reach my market?

- What is the transportation availability and what are the rates?

- What provisions for future expansion can I make:

- What is the topography of the site (slope and foundation)?

- What is the housing availability for workers and managers?

- What environmental factors (schools, cultural, community atmosphere) might affect my business and my employees?

- What will the quality of this site be in 5 years, 10 years, 25 years?

- What is my estimate of this site in relation to my major competitor?

- What other media are available for advertising? How many radio and television stations are there?

- Is the Quantity and quality of available labor concentrated in a given area in the city or town? If so, is commuting a way of living in that city or town?

- Is the city centrally located to my suppliers?

- What are the labor conditions, including such things as relationships with the business community and average wages and salaries paid?

- Is the local business climate healthy, or are business failures especially high in the area?

- What about tax requirements? Is there a city business tax? Income tax? What is the property tax rate? Is there a personal property tax? Are there other special taxes?

- Is the available police and fire protection adequate?

- Is the city or town basically well planned and managed in terms of such items as electric power, sewage, and paved streets and sidewalks?

Page A-8

Choosing the Proper Method of Organization

Listed below are legal forms of business available to the small business entrepreneur:

Sole Proprietorship

Advantages
- Simple to start
- All profits to owner
- Owner in direct control
- Easy entry and exit
- Taxed as individual

Disadvantages
- Unlimited liability
- "Jack-of-all-trades"
- Capital requirement limited
- Limited life
- Employee turn-over

Partnership

Advantages
- Easy to originate
- Credit rating
- Talent combination
- Legal Contract

Disadvantages
- Unlimited liability
- Misunderstandings
- Partner withdrawal
- Regulations

Corporation

Advantages
- Limited liability
- Expansion potential
- Transfer of ownership
- Retain employees

Disadvantages
- Double taxation
- Charter restrictions
- Employee motivation
- Legal regulations

What Is A Corporation?

A corporation is an artificial being, invisible, intangible, and existing only in contemplation of the law," wrote Chief Justice John Marshall. In other words, the corporation exists as a separate entity apart from its owners, the shareholders. It makes contracts; it is liable; it pays taxes. It is a "legal person".

The corporation is the most complex of the three major forms of business ownership. The corporation stands as a separate legal entity in the eyes of the law. The life of the corporation is independent of the owners' lives. Because the owners, called shareholders, are legally separate from the corporation, they can sell their interests in the business without affecting the continuation of the business. When a corporation is founded, it accepts the regulations and restrictions placed on it by the state in which it is incorporated and any other state in which it chooses to do business. Generally, the corporation must report its financial operations to the state's attorney general on an annual basis.

Estimating Start-up Costs

Item	Amount
Fixtures and Equipment	$ _____
Building & Land (If Needed)	_____
Store and/or Office Supplies	_____
Remodeling and Decorating	_____
Deposits on Utilities	_____
Insurance	_____
Installation of Fixtures	_____
Legal Fees	_____
Professional Fees	_____
Telephone	_____
Rental	_____
Salaries and Wages	_____
Inventory if Retailing	_____
Licenses and Permits	_____
Advertising and Promotion	_____
TOTAL Estimated Start-up Cost	$_____

Preparing An Income Statement

What is an Income Statement?

The income statement shows the income received and the expenses incurred over a period of time. Income received (sales) comes essentially from the sales of the merchandise or service which your business is formed to sell. Expenses incurred are the expired costs that have been incurred during the same period of time.

Plan A Budgeted Income Statement For One Year

1. Project Total Sales
2. Estimate Total Expenditures
3. Example Listed Below for Income Statement

Percents	1	2	3	4	5	6	7	8	9	10	11	12
Sales												
Cost of Sales												
Gross Profit												
Expenditure												
Rent Expense												
Supplies												
Wages/Salaries												
Utilities												
Insurance												
Depreciation												
Interest												
Miscellaneous												
Net Profit												

Preparing A Balance Sheet

What is a Balance Sheet?

The balance sheet shows the assets, liabilities and owner's net worth in a business as of a given date.

- Assets are the things owned by your business, including both physical things and claims against others.
- Liabilities are the amounts owned to others, the creditors of the firm.
- Net worth or owner's equity is the owner's claim to the assets after liabilities are accounted for.

A Budgeted Balance Sheet For One Year

- List all your business property at their cost to you: these are your assets.
- List all debts, or what your business owes on all your property; these are your liabilities.
- Take your total property balance (Assets), and subtract the total amount you owe (Liabilities).
- The balance is what you own in your business called (Owner's equity).
- Add Total Liabilities (2) & Total Owner's Equity (3).
- Listed on the next page is an example of a balance sheet.

NAME OF BUSINESS
BALANCE SHEET
DATE

ASSETS
Current Assets
  Cash   _____
  Accounts Receivable   _____
Merchandise Inventories   _____
    TOTAL CURRENT ASSETS   _____

Fixed Assets
  Land   _____
  Building   _____
  Equipment   _____
    TOTAL FIXED ASSETS   _____
      TOTAL ASSETS   1). _____

LIABILITIES
Current Liabilities
  Accounts Payable   _____
  Note Payable   _____
  Payroll Taxes Payable   _____
    TOTAL CURRENT LIABILITIES   _____

Long-term Liabilities
  Mortgage Payable   _____
  Long-term Note   _____
    TOTAL LONG-TERM LIABILITIES   _____
      TOTAL LIABILITIES   2). _____

OWNER'S EQUITY
Proprietor's Capital   3). _____

    TOTAL LIABILITIES & OWNER'S EQUITY   (2 &3). _____

Marketing The Business

1. Define Your Market
   • Type of Customers
   • Age, Income, Occupation of your customers
   • Type of Trading Area

2. Promotion of Your Business
   • Advertising
   • Setting your Image

3. Customer Policy Plan
   • Develop a Customer Profile
   • Customer Services
   • Customer Needs

4. Pricing Your Products/Services
   • Know all your Costs
   • Know your Profit Margin
   • Know Competitor's Price
   • Know what Return you want on your Investment

5. Sales Promotion
   • Coupons   • Demonstrations
   • Contests   • Giveaways
   • Displays   • Banners

6. Public Relations
   • Newspaper Article   • Radio Promotion
   • Contact Trade Association • TV Promotion

7. Segmentation of your Market
   • Age   • Location
   • Occupation   • Education
   • Income   • Hobbies

Marketing Planning

Outline for Marketing

I.   Product/Service Concept:
   a. Name of product or service
   b. Descriptive characteristics of product or service
   c. Unit sales
   d. Analysis of market trends

II. Number of Customers in your Market Area:
   a. Profile of customers
   b. Average customer expenditure
   c. Total market

III. Your Market Potential:
   a. Total market divided by competition
   b. Total market multiplied by percent who will buy your product

IV. Needs of Customers:
   a. Identification
   b. Pleasure
   c. Social approval
   d. Personal interest
   e. Price

V.   Direct Marketing Sources:
   a. Trade magazines
   b. Trade associations
   c. Small Business Administration (SBA)
   d. Government Publications
   e. Yellow pages
   f. Marketing directories

VI   Customer Profile:
   a. Geographical
   b. Gender
   c. Age range
   d. Income brackets
   e. Occupation
   f. Educational level

Advertising Media

Medium	Market Coverage	Type of Audience
Daily newspaper	Single community or entire metro area: zoned editions sometimes available	General
Weekly newspaper	Single Community	Residents
Telephone Directory	Geographical area or occupational field served by the directory	Active shoppers for goods or services
Direct mail audience	Controlled by the advertiser	Controlled
Radio audience	Definable market area	Selected
Television audience	Definable market area surrounding TV Stations	Various
Outdoor	Entire metro area	General auto drivers
Magazine	Entire metro area or magazine region	Selected audience

Management and Getting the Work Done

1. Define your objective for starting your business.

2. Define your goals: profit growth for first three years.

3. Develop an organization chart of your business.

4. Define your personal needs.
   - Hiring proper employees
   - Training employees
   - Motivation

5. Define all responsibility for each person in your business.

6. Define all authority.
   - Who will hire and fire?
   - Who will select and train all personnel?
   - Who will keep the important records as to inventory, purchasing, sales records, cash records, etc.?

7. Define all laws and regulations that will be requirements for operating your business.

8. Review all duties and tasks with all your employees.

9. Write a summary of all the important tasks that you want to finish in your first year in business.

Sample Organization Chart

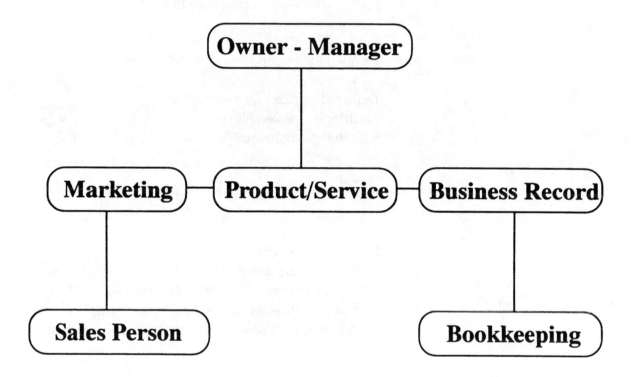

Summary of The Business Plan

Name of Business
BUSINESS PLAN
Date

1. Define your business
   - Name all principals
   - Address and phone number

2. Define your products or services

3. Define your market

4. Define your site or location

5. Advertising Plan
   - Budget
   - Media

6. Chart of Start-up cost

7. Worksheet of Income Statement
   - Revenue/Income
   - Expenses

8. Worksheet of Balance Sheet
   - Assets (Property)
   - Capital (Owner's Equity)
   - Liabilities (Debts)

9. Personnel Outline
   - Number of Employees
   - Staffing & Training

10. Management Organization
    - Organization Chart
    - Evaluation Policy
    - Job Profile

11. Special Statement
    - 3-Year Sales Schedule
    - Cash Flow
    - 3-Year Expense Schedule

Appendix A Summary

1. Contact your State Commerce Department for guidelines in starting your business.

2. Contact your City/County Clerk for guidelines in starting your business.

3. Contact all other Governmental Centers that will furnish you all the legal regulations and tax laws that will effect your business.
   - State Government
   - Internal Revenue Service
   - State Employment Security Commission
   - Department of Treasury
   - City Governmental Units

        a. Fire
        b. Police
        c. Zoning
        d. Building Permits
        e. Health
        f. Water & Sewage

4. Township Government
   - Local Legal Requirements
   - Local Taxes
   - Local Health Permits
   - Local Zoning Laws

Reference Materials

Management Aids Titles

Contact the

**Small Business Administration
P.O. Box 15434
Fort Worth, TX 76119**

for the following booklets:

- Number 2.025   Thinking About Going Into Business
- Number 2.010   Planning and Goal Setting For Business
- Number 1.016   Sound Cash Management
- Number 1.001   The A.B.C's. of Borrowing
- Number 1.008   Break-even Analysis
- Number 2.022   Business Plan For Service Firms
- Number 2.023   Business Plans for Retail Firms

Notes _____

Appendix B

HOUSEHOLD NEEDS

Many small business start-ups fail due to their inability to support their owners. Rarely do new businesses support their owners from the start. However, many individuals fail to recognize this fact. In addition, then, to a sound business plan, it is necessary for an owner to project the household cash needs month-by-month for the first three years of the business' operation. As a new business owner, you should be able to support yourself until your new business is able to support you in a manner to which you are accustomed.

MONTHLY HOUSEHOLD CASH NEEDS

Regular NON-BUSINESS Income
Spouse's salary
Investment income
Social security
Other income
Retirement benefits
Less taxes
Net monthly income

Regular Monthly Expenses

Housing
    Mortgage/Rent
    Utilities
    Homeowner's insurance
    Property taxes
    Home repairs

Living Expenses
    Groceries
    Telephone
    Tuition
    Transportation
    Meals
    Child care
    Medical expenses
    Clothing
    Personal

Insurance Premiums
    Life insurance
    Disability insurance
    Auto insurance
    Medical insurance

Debt Repayment
    Auto loans
    Consumer debt

Discretionary Expenses
    Entertainment
    Vacation
    Gifts _____
    Retirement contributions
    Investment savings
    Charitable contributions
    Dues, magazines, etc.
    Professional fees
    Other

Total Monthly Expenses

Monthly Surplus/Deficit

Total Year Surplus/Deficit
(Monthly x 12)

Available Assets to Cover Deficit
    Checking accounts
    Savings accounts
    Money market accounts
    Personal credit lines
    Marketable securities
    Lump-sum retirement/
      severance
    Other assets

Total Assets

NEEDED RESERVES
    Total Assets-Deficit

PERSONAL FINANCIAL STATEMENT

This is a picture of your personal financial condition to date. It is a very important part of any loan application and/or interview, especially when a loan for a projected new business is under consideration.

PERSONAL FINANCIAL STATEMENT

_____ _____ , 19 _____

Assets
Cash _____
Savings accounts _____
Stocks, bonds, other securities _____
Accounts/Notes receivable _____
Life insurance cash value _____
Rebates/Refunds _____
Autos/Other vehicles _____
Real estate _____
Vested pension plan/Retirement accounts _____
Other assets _____

TOTAL ASSETS $ _____

Liabilities

Accounts payable _____
Contracts payable _____
Notes payable _____
Taxes _____
Real estate loans _____
Other liabilities _____

TOTAL LIABILITIES $ _____

TOTAL ASSETS $ _____

LESS TOTAL LIABILITIES $ _____

NET WORTH $ _____

BALANCE SHEET

A balance sheet is a current financial statement. It is a dollars and cents description of your business (existing or projected) which lists all of its assets and liabilities.

BALANCE SHEET

_____ _____ , 19 _____

	YEAR 1	YEAR II
Current Assets		
Cash	_____	_____
Accounts receivable	_____	_____
Inventory	_____	_____
Fixed Assets		
Real estate	_____	_____
Fixtures and equipment	_____	_____
Vehicles	_____	_____
Other Assets		
License	_____	_____
Goodwill	_____	_____
TOTAL ASSETS	$_____	$_____
Current Liabilities		
Notes payable (due within 1 year)	$_____	$_____
Accounts payable	_____	_____
Accrued expenses	_____	_____
Taxes owed	_____	_____
Long-Term Liabilities		
Notes payable (due after 1 year)	_____	_____
Other	_____	_____
TOTAL LIABILITIES	$_____	$_____
NETWORTH (ASSETS minus LIABILITIES)	$_____	$_____

TOTAL LIABILITIES plus NET WORTH should equal ASSETS

PROFIT AND LOSS STATEMENT

A profit and loss statement is a detailed earnings statement for the previous full year (if you are already in business). Existing businesses are also required to show a profit and loss statement for the current period to the date of the balance sheet.

PROJECTED PROFIT AND LOSS STATEMENT

	Month 1	Month 2	Month 3	Month 4	Month 5	Month 6	Month 7	Month 8	Month 9	Month 10	Month 11	Month 12
Total Net Sales												
Cost of Sales												
GROSS PROFIT												
Controllable Expenses												
Salaries												
Payroll taxes												
Security												
Advertising												
Automobile												
Dues and subscriptions												
Legal and accounting												
Office supplies												
Telephone												
Utilities												
Miscellaneous												
Total Controllable Expenses												
Fixed Expenses Depreciation												
Insurance												
Rent												
Taxes and licenses												
Loan payments												
Total Fixed Expenses												
TOTAL EXPENSES												
NET PROFIT (LOSS) (before taxes)												

CASH FLOW PROJECTIONS

A cash flow projection is a forcast of the cash (checks or money orders) a business anticipates receiving and disbursing during the course of a month. Well managed, the cash flow should be sufficient to meet the cash requirements for the following month.

CASH FLOW PROJECTIONS

	Start-up or prior to loan	Month 1	Month 2	Month 3	Month 4	Month 5	Month 6	Month 7	Month 8	Month 9	Month 10	Month 11	Month 12	TOTAL
Cash (beginning of month														
Cash on hand														
Cash in bank														
Cash in investments														
Total Cash														
Income (during month)														
Cash sales														
Credit sales payment														
Investment income														
Loans														
Other cash income														
Total Income														
TOTAL CASH AND INCOME														
Expenses (during month														
Inventory or new material														
Wages (including owner's)														
Taxes														
Equipment expense														
Overhead														
Selling expense														
Transportation														
Loan repayment														
Other cash expenses														
TOTAL EXPENSES														
CASH FLOW EXCESS (end of month)														
CASH FLOW CUMULATIVE (Monthly)														

Getting Down to Business...

How to Start & Manage A Plumbing Services Business

An Instructional Guide for Creating A Small Business
by Jerre G. Lewis, M.A.
& Leslie D. Renn, M.S.

Notes

Planning a Plumbing Business

Goal: To help you plan your plumbing business.

Objective 1: Describe the services, customers,
and competition of a plumbing business.

Objective 2: List three helpful personal qualities
an owner of a plumbing business might have.

Objective 3: List three ways to help
your business compete successfully.

Objective 4: List one or more special legal requirements
for running a plumbing business.

Notes _____

Planning a Plumbing Business

There are many, many small businesses in America. Small businesses can have as few as one worker (the owner) or as many as four workers. A small business owner is "self-employed." Often a whole family works together in a small business.

Most plumbers work for someone else as an employee. But some plumbers work independently and are self-employed. Others may hire employees and become an owner-manager. These materials can help you learn what is involved in being self-employed. Then you can decide if it is a long-term career goal you would like for yourself.

In this section you will learn about these four things involved in planning a plumbing business:

- deciding what the services, customers, and competition will be;

- deciding what personal skills and characteristics are needed for this type of business;

- deciding what to do to compete successfully; and

- learning about the legal requirements for running this type of business.

Services, Customers, and Competition

An important step in planning is to decide what services you will offer, who your customers will be, and what the competition offers.

Services. There are several types of plumbing services that can be provided. Some companies specialize in one area. Others provide a range of services. One service area is to do construction work and install the plumbing in a new building. Another type of service is to remodel or replace plumbing. For example, a home owner may call in a plumber to modernize a bathroom or replace a sink. A third major area is to clean or repair the plumbing or replace small equipment. Often drains and water lines collect sludge or grease and need to be cleaned out. Repairs are often needed. These range from a leaky faucet to a broken water line. Equipment may need to be fixed or replaced. It could be a garbage disposal or a water heater.

Customers. General contractors are good customers for new construction work in homes and other buildings. General contractors may also be customers for remodeling work. Home owners are potential customers for drain cleaning, repair work, and remodeling. Other potential customers are apartment owners and owners of small businesses, such as restaurants or stores. Factories and office buildings also need services. These include construction, remodeling, repair, and maintenance services.

Competition. There is competition in the plumbing business. Some companies are large and provide a wide range of services. Other businesses specialize in a type of service such as underground water pipes or small repair. There are some plumbing companies that have several branches, especially in the area of drain and sewer cleaning. Each business offers a service they believe people need and will pay for.

Personal Qualities

You want to know if you have the personal qualities that are needed to run your own business. You know you have the necessary skills in your craft. You learned about business laws for your license test. Below are personal qualities that may be important.

Like people. You feel it is important to like dealing with both customers and employees.

Be a good organizer and planner. You feel it is important to be organized and to be able to plan your time and your work. You also know it is important to pay attention to details.

Have good business sense. You know you must know about costs and decide how much to charge. That way you can make a profit and yet not charge more than your competition.

Be a problem solver. You know that customers will call you with a problem. Your job is to help solve these problems.

Be a hard worker. You know it will take hard work. You will probably work longer hours than at your old job.

How to Compete Successfully

There are several things you can do to compete successfully. We will mention them now, and you will learn more about them as you work through the materials.

Do a lot of research and planning before you start the business. This will help you to decide what services to offer and where to offer these services. You should offer a service you think people want and will pay for.

Offer special services that other businesses do not offer. For example, you could offer 24-hour response to emergency calls.

Establish a business image that people will remember. You may want an image that is professional, yet friendly.

Legal Requirements

The laws for starting a plumbing business vary from state to state. Most states require that you have several years of experience, pass a state test, and demonstrate your financial reliability to qualify for a contractor's license. Once you have your contractor's license, then you can start your own business. You will usually need a city business license, also, you will have to find out exactly what the legal requirements are in your local area.

Summary

Plumbing businesses do new construction, remodeling, repair, and maintenance work. They provide services for homes, apartments, small businesses, and commercial buildings. In new construction, they work as a subcontractor for a general contractor. The small business owner should be good at his or her trade and also good at running a business.

Notes

Choosing a Location

Goal: To help you choose a location for a plumbing business.

Objective 1: List three things to think about in deciding
on a service area for your business.

Objective 2: Pick the best location for a plumbing business
from three choices and explain your choice.

Notes

Choosing a Location

There are several things to think about when you choose a service area for your business. You should consider these factors.

- Are there enough customers in this area?

- What is the competition?

- Is this where I want to work?

You will also need to decide on a specific location for your shop and office. These are things to think about.

Customers

- Is this enough space?

- Can I afford the rent?

- Is the building in good condition?

- Is the location convenient?

The housing mix, income level, growth trends, and economic conditions of the area are important in deciding where to locate and what services to provide. Older homes generally have more repair, maintenance, and replacement work. People owning houses in a high economic area may spend more for remodeling or replacement than those in a low-income area. An area where new houses or new businesses are being built is a good location to do new construction work.

General economic conditions and the availability of money to finance building are also important in new construction. Repair work tends to be more even. But the amount of new construction work may be unstable. Trade magazines and business publications are good sources of information on the age of houses and growth patterns.

Competition

You must also consider the other businesses in the area that provide this service. You can find out how many there are by looking at the Yellow Pages. You should also consider the size of the business. A person working alone or a small business would not provide the same competition as a large operation. Also consider what services these businesses provide. Perhaps you are offering a new or better service. There are a number of things to learn about regarding the competition. Talking to other people in the trades in your local area is a good way to find out about these things.

Balance Between Customers and Competition

What is important is the number of customers in relation to the people offering this service. You feel that there was enough work in your area to support yourself. You also feel you are aiming at a different market- single-family homes—than the big plumbing companies.

Personal Considerations

There are other things to consider about the location. You might ask, "Is this where I want to work? Is this where I want to start a business?" People often have personal reasons for deciding where to start their businesses. These reasons include family or friends. You want to work in your town where you have contacts in the construction industry.

Selecting a Specific Location

Sometimes a plumber can start a small business from his or her home.

It depends on whether it is legal where they live. The plumber can use space in the house for an office and use the garage for storage. The plumber may hire an answering service to take his or her calls.

A larger operation would include a shop, storage area, a garage for trucks, and an office. The business would be located in an area zoned for commercial or industrial use. Customers would not usually come to the office. Rather, the owner would talk to them on the telephone. Or the owner might go to their homes or businesses to discuss and do the work.

The building should be clean and in good condition. Also, it is important that the shop be close to the jobs. Otherwise a lot of time may be spent in travel. The business may include selling plumbing parts, or it may have a showroom with fixtures. Then the customers would come to the shop. In this case, appearance and nearness to potential customers would be important. The business owner has to weigh the advantages of having a shop and office against the expense of renting the space.

Summary

To decide on a service area, you must consider if there is enough business in the area to support a new plumbing business. In selecting a specific office space, you must decide how much you can afford and if the space location and condition of the building meet your needs.

Notes

Being in Charge

Owning your own plumbing business may involve hiring and supervising other people. This unit will discuss:

- tasks and the skills needed to do them;

- hiring staff; and

- keeping employees happy.

Tasks

Here are some typical tasks in a plumbing business and the background required for each of them.

Managing tasks. These tasks include organizing the work, scheduling, making decisions, training and supervising employees, organizing financial information, planning, customer relations, promotion, handling business details, purchasing, getting permits, and staying up to date on codes. With respect to background, it is important to have knowledge in the technical aspects of plumbing, experience in supervising others, and business skills.

Estimating tasks. These tasks include making estimates of how much ; job will cost, talking to customers about what they want and how much they will pay, and negotiating with customers on the price for a job. With respect to background, it is important to know how long different tasks take, be able to find the price for required parts, and be skilled in dealing with customers.

Doing the plumbing work. These tasks involve all kinds of plumbing, including new residential construction, new commercial construction, remodeling, repair work, or cleaning lines. Certain background and skills are required. You should have basic training and experience in the specific area. Large jobs may involve more specialization or supervisory responsibilities. Repair work would require skills in dealing with customers.

<u>Office work</u>. These tasks include typing, bookkeeping, filing, recordkeeping, and answering telephones. With respect to background, you should have basic typing, office procedures classes, or similar experience.

You plan on doing the managing, estimating, and office work, as well as doing most of the plumbing. You hire an assistant to help with the plumbing tasks. Larger companies are more specialized. They may employ many plumbers as well as people who serve as supervisors, estimators, and office workers.

Choosing Workers

Good workers are important to the success of a business. To select a good employee, you should plan what tasks need to be done. Then recruit the right employee for those teaks.

The best way to recruit depends on your local area. Some sources new employees are:

- unions and trade associations;

- suggestions of friends;

- schools and training programs;

- the U.S. Employment Office; and

- want ads in the local newspapers.

Some employers hire through the union. They tell the union how many workers they need and any special skills required. They may want a journeyman or an apprentice. The union will then dispatch a worker from its list of available people. The employer can recall a former worker. Or the employer may be able occasionally to request a specific person. The minimum wages and benefits are set by the union. The employer who hires through the union knows that the worker has met certain skill requirements. It is important to check with the local union on its policies.

Other employers hire non-union plumbers. Often they can pay the employee a lower wage than if they hired a union member. However, they may find it difficult to find a well-trained non-union plumber. Also, they will probably not be able to work on jobs that hire other union workers.

To hire office help, you should write a job description and advertise the position. You will want applicants to fill out an application and have a personal interview. You should look for someone who has the skills required, is reliable, and wants to do the job.

Keeping People Happy

Once you've hired your employees, it's important to keep them happy. That way they will do quality work and continue on the job. Some of the ways to do this are: good pay and benefits, clear policies, clear directions, appropriate training, and good personal relations.

Pay. The pay and benefits you give your employees should be close to what they would get working for someone else. If you pay less, they may get a job elsewhere. If you pay much more, you may not be able to keep your prices low enough to be competitive. If you are a union shop, their pay may be set already. Then you will pay a minimum union rate. A bonus for work well done or other monetary incentives can motivate your employees.

Clear policies. You should be aware of labor laws regarding pay, overtime, and other work conditions and follow these laws. You should be clear on what your policies are. Communicate what they are to your employees. You may decide to offer emergency plumbing repair service. Then you will want to make arrangements for someone to be willing to work evenings and weekends to respond to calls.

Clear directions. The clearer you can be with your employees about what you expect, the more likely they will do it. Some things you will want done a certain way. Your employees aren't mind readers. You need to be clear on how you want things done. In other areas you may want to allow your employees to use their own judgment. In those cases you should support your employees' decisions. Tell them if you want something done differently in the future.

Appropriate training You should know what your staff is capable of and give them training when needed. You may hire experienced workers. Even so, you should start out by supervising them closely and checking their work. Then you can give them more independence. Also you can assign them to jobs that are appropriate to their skill level. You can also teach them new skills. Appropriate training and supervision will benefit your employees and maintain the quality of the work. You can also encourage employees to take available training classes. That way they will learn new skills and keep current on new developments in your field.

<u>Good personal relations</u>. As the owner, you should talk with your employees. Learn what concerns they may have and be sure they are clear on what you expect. Recognition of work well done can promote good working relationships. Working as a supervisor is a good way of learning these skills for managing employees.

The attitude of the owner and how the owner relates to the staff set the tone of the business. The owner may be positive, productive, fair, and may enjoy the work. This can create the kind of company that people want to work for. On the other hand, the owner may be unorganized, inconsistent, overly critical, or lax in supervision. This can create a negative atmosphere and employee dissatisfaction. The owner sets the standards and can be key in influencing the attitude of workers.

Summary
There are many tasks involved in a plumbing business. The owner should be clear on what the tasks are and select appropriate people to do them. The way the owner manages is key to setting the atmosphere for a business.

Organizing the Work

In a plumbing business you must organize the work, do the work, and check the work. That way you make sure it was done well and that the customer is satisfied. It is important to set up a system so employees know what needs to be done, when it must be done, and who will do it. The system should be flexible and allow for changes. For example, one job may be delayed because needed parts are not available or due to bad weather. Any system should allow for making adjustments when needed.

The Work Order

The work order is used to record the customer's order and to request that the workers do the work. Some work orders may be filled out over the telephone or by the worker when the work is done. This would be done for service work or small repair jobs. It is different for a larger job, such as a construction or a major remodeling job. Someone will inspect the job first and make a detailed estimate. Then the person will use this information to prepare a work order or contract.

The work order is important in describing what work should be done and who should do it. The customers get a copy of the work done for their records. It is important that the work order be filled out carefully and completely. That way there is an accurate record of the work. This can be very important in cases of misunderstandings with customers about what is to be done and the cost.

On the next page is a sample work order for a commercial installation job.

WORK ORDER

FROM: _____ Aardvark Plumbing _____   DATE: _____ 8/1 _____

_____ 5673 Frontage Road _____   WORK ORDER NUMBER: _____ 81 _____

_____ Centerville, Oregon _____   ORDER TAKEN BY: _____ Leroy _____

WORK FOR: _____ Harry's Deli _____   START WORK ON: _____ 8/4/82 _____

_____ 620 Market Street _____   FINISH WORK ON: _____ 8/5/82 _____

_____ Centerville, Oregon _____

_____   TERMS OF PAYMENT: _____ Cash _____

Person Doing Work	Description of Work	Materials	Labor	Total Cost
Frank	Install 2 stainless steel sinks	583.00	321.00	

WORK FINISHED ON: _____ 8/5 _____   TOTAL MATERIALS USED: 583.00

BY: _____ Frank _____   TOTAL LABOR 321.00

TAX (5%) 29.15

TOTAL COST: 933.15

Contracts

A contract is used for larger jobs. A contract includes:

- the names of the people involved;

- what services will be provided;

- when they will be performed;

- how much it will cost;

- how it will be paid for; and

- other appropriate information.

Sometimes the customer pays when the job is complete. Sometimes they pay in installments as stages of the work are completed. A clear contract is important for the protection of all parties.

Scheduling

Someone must plan the work. She or he must decide in what order it should be done and who should do it. There are a number of things to consider in coordinating work. First, you need to know how important it is that the work be done soon. You would want to place jobs such as unclogging a kitchen sink before a routine maintenance job. A close estimate of how long a job will take is helpful. Second, you need to know the skills of all workers. You also need to know when they will be available to do the work they specialize in. Grouping together jobs in the same part of town can increase efficiency. Third, in new construction, you must plan for the delivery of parts and coordinate your work with the other contractors. So the person doing the scheduling must juggle different things. The person also needs to be flexible and to allow for the unexpected. This could include a call from a good customer who is having a plumbing emergency.

It is important for good customer relations to do the work as scheduled and to keep appointments. There may be a change in the schedule. Then it is important to consult with the customer first and to inform him or her of last-minute changes.

Below is a sample work schedule for one day. The work schedule lists the name of each employee. It also shows the work to be done that day in the order it should be done. In this case, jobs are described by work order numbers. On April 6 Hank and James worked together on a two-person job on the first assignment.

WORK SCHEDULE

DATE: <u>Monday, April 6</u>

Employee	Description of Job
Hank	$104, #101, #105
James	#104, Start Campbell job, #100

Each worker may also receive a written work schedule for the day. Often the person doing the scheduling will want to communicate with employees during the day. This can be done by having:

- employees return to the office after each job;

- employees call in during the day;

- a wireless paging system; or even

- a radio communication system.

Time Planning

A major problem for most small business owners is planning their own time. Owners tend to work long hours, especially when they start the business. There are a number of ways to improve your use of time. One way is to list all the things you want to do. Then rank them in order of importance. Take into consideration both how important they are and when they should be done.

A written schedule is also helpful. Make reasonable time estimates and allow time for the unexpected. Also, many people find it easier to stick to a schedule if they include time for doing those things they enjoy doing. Often in making up a written schedule a person will find that there just isn't time to do everything. Then he or she must make choices and accept that some things on their list just won't get done. At that point, they may find they need to talk to other people and change agreements on getting some things done or delegate work to other employees.

You may find that things go more smoothly when you don't schedule the work too tightly. Then you can be more flexible in adjusting to changes.

Summary

A plumbing business needs a system for recording work orders and scheduling the work. Carefully planning and good communication are important for a smooth operation.

Appendix D

INSURANCE CHECKLIST

TYPE OF INSURANCE	PURCHASE	DO NOT PURCHASE
PROPERTY INSURANCE:		
Fire	_____	_____
Windstorm	_____	_____
Hail	_____	_____
Smoke	_____	_____
Explosion	_____	_____
Vandalism	_____	_____
Water Damage	_____	_____
Glass	_____	_____
LIABILITY INSURANCE	_____	_____
WORKERS' COMPENSATION	_____	_____
BUSINESS INTERRUPTION	_____	_____
DISHONESTY:		
Fidelity	_____	_____
Robbery	_____	_____
Burglary	_____	_____
Comprehensive	_____	_____
PERSONAL:		
Health	_____	_____
Life	_____	_____
Key Personnel	_____	_____

Special Appendix

Web Site Marketing

Business Web Site
an
Effective Marketing Tool

More than 100 million people use the Internet each day. A website offers help in marketing your small business. Your web site can help level the playing field for small businesses who compete with big businesses. It can enable small business to expand their business nationally or internationally.

What makes a good web site?

A good web site shows by doing; it proves rather than states. Instead of making claims, it provides evidence.

Evidence can take several forms:

- Case Studies showing how your efforts solved a previous client's problems.

- Testimonials from satisfied clients.

- Reprints of articles you've written or reviews of your work.

Education, however, remains the best way to establish credibility. To the extent prospects leave your web site better informed about your product or service, the easier it is to gain their respect (and their purchase order).

Three steps to creating your own business web site.

Today's tools make web publishing accessible to small businesses without programming experience. For example, Microsoft® Publisher 97 includes PageWizard design assistants, web deign elements and design checkers to help your build a workable web site.

Step one:

Choose a structure and a look. Your site should be structured and designed to best tell your story. But where do you start? Using the Page Wizard, you can choose from pre-designed options that can later be customized so that establishing a structure and "look" is easy.

Step two:

Tell your story. Next, simply select the sample headlines and text provided and replace them with words that describe what you have to offer.

Step three:

Check your work and post your site. The design in Publisher 97 goes through your web site element by element, identifying potential problems. Then, the web publishing wizard guides you through the process of posting your web site on the local Internet service provider or on-line service of your choice.

Remember, with millions of web sites, you may have to market your web site as well as your small business to get traffic for your business. The web site can be an inexpensive way of effectively building your small business.

10 tips for Web Site Online Marketing

1. Put up a simple web page.
2. Use a name that will attract people
3. Give away advice and information
4. Have lots of e-mail correspondence
5. Provide customized pages for users.
6. Visit user groups
7. Get on mailing lists
8. Arrange links with related sites
9. Make sure you're in every possible directory
10. Do not "SPAM"

The principals of a Website

In today's business world, a good website is essential to any advertising campaign, but you need to understand, that all websites are not created equal. Nearly any web development company can build you a site that looks good, but if the public cannot locate it, does it really exist?

First off you need to understand that websites are only limited by your imagination, but again I stress, no matter how creative, how interactive, or how great it looks, if the public cannot easily find it, what good is it? Each search engine has created a list of criteria that your site must comply with, in order to be placed in the top 10 listings; this criteria list varies from search engine to search engine and is not made public.

Optimization; The first three rules of any business also applies to websites; location, location, location. 85% of all internet users use the search engines to find what they are looking for.

Nearly 85% of all searches performed in the world go through Google, Yahoo, and MSN, with AOL at a distant 4th with about 8%. This means that the thousands of other search engines share the last 7 to 10%. Less than 3% of the public will search past the 3rd page, therefore it is imperative for your website to work, it must have top rankings!

The 10 second rule; the average internet user will search through 7 sites before finding what they are looking for. Once your site is located, you have approximately 10 seconds to entice the visitor to go deeper into your site. To accomplish this, your home page needs to provide a brief summary of your site. The visitor must be able to scan this page and conclude that your site contains the information they are seeking within that 10 second window. You can always test the success of your home page by checking your web stats and comparing the visitors to pages viewed. If the average is 2 pages per visitor or better, than you know the average visitor likes what they see.

Contact Info; Studies have shown that the average internet user would rather contact you by telephone than by email whenever possible, yet many websites do not contain a phone number or it is buried in the contact us page. A good website will make the contact information available on every page. If your site is intended to be fully automated, then at least display a "take an action" link prominently on each page.

Newsletters; Electronic newsletters are greatly overlooked. A good monthly newsletter will keep your business at the front of their thoughts. Always be sure the newsletter contains a quick link to your website.

As I previously stated, any web company can make a site look good, but only a few websites have the potential to work, to actually tell your story and bring in business.

Although you can buy a website development program, and possibly build your own site, the odds are greatly stacked against you. Less than one thousandth of one percent of the websites out there can be easily located. Another important tip is to hire a company that not only specializes in regional or global optimization (depending upon your market area), but a company that offers an all inclusive annual program with options for future years at a guaranteed renewal price. I have provided the following link to Sutherland's Web Services, (www.sws.tc). SWS, is a good example of an all inclusive, web development firm that specializes in regional optimization. The all inclusive services of Sutherland's includes; hosting, maintenance, updates, design, development, programming and support. Always remember; "If your site cannot be located, does it really exist?

Stephen H. Sutherland
Sutherland's Web Services
www.sws.tc
Steve@sws.tc
231-929-2655

INDEX

Step-by-Step Guides
To Start, Manage & Market
Your Own Business

4th Printing!

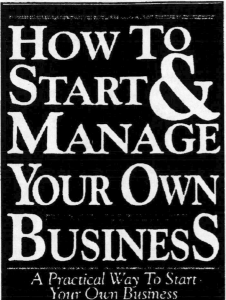

**How To Start & Manage
Your Own Business**

For anyone who is looking to start-up a new business, this *step-by-step guide* includes planning, managing, marketing and promotion.

$21.95

Soft Cover • 104 Pages
5 1/2" x 8 1/2" 0-9628759-0-2 ©1992

New!

How to Start & Manage a **Home Based** Business

A Practical Way to Start Your Own Business

by

Jerre G. Lewis and Leslie D. Renn

**How to Start & Manage
a Home Based Business**

This book provides the knowledge and tools necessary to successfully plan, design, and start up a new business in a practical way. With a step-by-step guide for planning, managing, marketing and promotion of a small business, in an easy-to-read and easy-to-understand format. The guidelines presented will help you pursue dreams of independence and financial success.

$21.95

Soft Cover • 135 Pages
5 1/2" x 8 1/2" 1-887005-11-0 © 1996

3rd Printing!

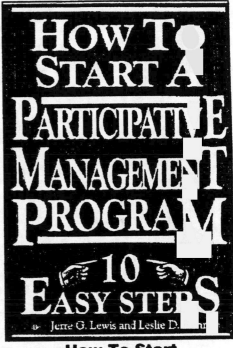

**How To Start
A Participative
Management Program**

A concise guide for small to midsize companies that is easy to read and follow *Step-by-step planning, managing and marketing of a small business* • How to empower and involve employees • Contains tools for measuring employees work environment.

$21.95

Soft Cover • 93 Pages •
5 1/2" x 8 1/2", 0-9628759 ©1992

ABOUT THE AUTHORS
Jerre G. Lewis and Leslie D. Renn are both experienced professionals concerning small business management and entrepreneurship. For more than twenty years Mr. Lewis has been involved with business education at college level and the development of a series of small business seminars. He is a Certified Education Specialist for the U.S. Small Business Administration Volunteer Counseling Program. Mr. Renn is a business owner, entrepreneur, a small business consultant, and like Mr. Lewis, is involved with college level management instruction & business seminars. He also has extensive experience in large industry administration. Mr. Lewis and Mr. Renn received bachelors and masters degrees from Michigan universities, and both work and live in northern Michigan.

Business Books

Telephone 1-231-275-7287 • Fax 1-231-275-7242 • lewisjv@centurytel.net
Telephone 1-480-807-9530 • Fax 1-480-830-1187 • lrenn@cox.net

NEW EDITION 2007

How to Start and Manage:

ISBN	Title
ISBN 978-1-57916-152-1	An Apparel Store Business
ISBN 978-1-57916-153-8	A Word Processing Service Business
ISBN 978-1-57916-154-5	A Garden Center Business
ISBN 978-1-57916-155-2	A Hair Styling Shop Business
ISBN 978-1-57916-156-9	A Bicycle Shop Business
ISBN 978-1-57916-157-6	A Travel Agency Business
ISBN 978-1-57916-158-3	An Answering Service Business
ISBN 978-1-57916-159-0	A Health Spa Business
ISBN 978-1-57916-160-6	A Restaurant Business
ISBN 978-1-57916-161-3	A Specialty Food Store Business
ISBN 978-1-57916-162-0	A Welding Business
ISBN 978-1-57916-163-7	A Day Care Center Business
ISBN 978-1-57916-164-4	A Flower and Plant Store Business
ISBN 978-1-57916-165-1	A Construction Electrician Business
ISBN 978-1-57916-166-8	A Housecleaning Service Business
ISBN 978-1-57916-167-5	A Nursing Service Business
ISBN 978-1-57916-168-2	A Bookkeeping Service Business
ISBN 978-1-57916-169-9	A Bed and Breakfast Business
ISBN 978-1-57916-170-5	A Secretarial Service Business
ISBN 978-1-57916-171-2	An Energy Specialist Business
ISBN 978-1-57916-172-9	A Guard Service Business
ISBN 978-1-57916-173-6	A Software Design Business
ISBN 978-1-57916-174-3	An Air Conditioning & Heating Business
ISBN 978-1-57916-175-0	A Plumbing Service Business
ISBN 978-1-57916-176-7	A Sewing Service Business
ISBN 978-1-57916-177-4	A Carpentry Service Business
ISBN 978-1-57916-178-1	A Home Attendent Service Business
ISBN 978-1-57916-179-8	A Tree Service Business
ISBN 978-1-57916-180-4	A Dairy Farming Business
ISBN 978-1-57916-181-1	A Farm Equipment Repair Service Business
ISBN 978-1-57916-182-8	A Children's Clothing Store Business
ISBN 978-1-57916-183-5	A Women's Apparel Store
ISBN 978-1-57916-184-2	A Convenience Food Store Business
ISBN 978-1-57916-185-9	A Pest Control Service Business
ISBN 978-1-57916-186-6	A Printing Business
ISBN 978-1-57916-187-3	An Ice Cream Business
ISBN 978-1-57916-188-0	A Mail Order Business
ISBN 978-1-57916-189-7	A Bookstore Business
ISBN 978-1-57916-190-3	A Home Furnishing Business
ISBN 978-1-57916-191-0	A Retail Florist Business
ISBN 978-1-57916-192-7	A Radio-Television Repair Shop Business
ISBN 978-1-57916-193-4	A Dry Cleaning Business
ISBN 978-1-57916-194-1	A Hardware Store Business
ISBN 978-1-57916-195-8	A Marine Retailing Business
ISBN 978-1-57916-196-5	An Office Products Business
ISBN 978-1-57916-197-2	A Pharmacy Business
ISBN 978-1-57916-198-9	A Fish Farming Business
ISBN 978-1-57916-199-6	A Personal Referral Service Business
ISBN 978-1-57916-200-9	A Solar Energy Business
ISBN 978-1-57916-201-6	A Building Service Contracting Business
ISBN 978-1-57916-202-3	A Retail Decorating Products Business
ISBN 978-1-57916-203-0	A Sporting Goods Store Business
ISBN 978-1-57916-204-7	A Retail Grocery Store
ISBN 978-1-57916-205-4	A Cosmetology Business
ISBN 978-1-57916-206-1	A Franchised Business
ISBN 978-1-57916-207-8	An Electronics Industry Consulting Practice Business
ISBN 978-1-57916-208-5	An Independent Consulting Practice Business
ISBN 978-1-57916-209-2	An Independent Trucking Business
ISBN 978-1-57916-210-8	An Accounting Service Business
ISBN 978-1-57916-211-5	A Nursery Business
ISBN 978-1-57916-212-2	A Seminar Promotion Business
ISBN 978-1-57916-231-9	A Bar & Cocktail Lounge Business
ISBN 978-1-57916-214-6	A Wheelchair Transportation Business
ISBN 978-1-57916-215-3	A Fertilizer and Pesticide Business
ISBN 978-1-57916-216-0	A Desktop Publishing Business
ISBN 978-1-57916-217-7	A Crime Prevention Business
ISBN 978-1-57916-218-4	A Gift Shop Business
ISBN 978-1-57916-219-1	A Handcraft Success Business
ISBN 978-1-57916-220-7	A Coin-Operated Laundries Business
ISBN 978-1-57916-221-4	A Property Management Business
ISBN 978-1-57916-222-1	An Auto Supply Store Business
ISBN 978-1-57916-223-8	A Men's Apparel Store Business
ISBN 978-1-57916-224-5	A Temporary Help Service Business
ISBN 978-1-57916-225-2	An Advertising Agency Business
ISBN 978-1-57916-226-9	A Firewood Sales Business
ISBN 978-1-57916-227-6	A Children's Bookstore Business
ISBN 978-1-57916-228-3	A Used Bookstore Business
ISBN 978-1-57916-229-0	A Sandwich Shop Deli Business
ISBN 978-1-57916-230-6	An Instant Print/Copy Shop
ISBN 978-1-57916-231-3	A Gift Specialty Store Business
ISBN 978-1-57916-232-0	A Gift Basket Service Business
ISBN 978-1-57916-233-7	A Hospitality Management Business
ISBN 978-1-57916-234-4	A Hotel Business
ISBN 978-1-57916-235-1	A Catering Service Business
ISBN 978-1-57916-236-8	A Carpet-Cleaning Service Business
ISBN 978-1-57916-237-5	A Window-Washing Service Business
ISBN 978-1-57916-238-2	An Innkeeping Service Business
ISBN 978-1-57916-239-9	An Apartment Preparation Service
ISBN 978-1-57916-240-5	A Kiosks and Cart Business
ISBN 978-1-57916-241-2	A Janitorial Service Business
ISBN 978-1-57916-242-9	A Medical Claims Processing Business
ISBN 978-1-57916-243-6	A Nursing Home Care Business
ISBN 978-1-57916-244-3	A Home Health Care Business
ISBN 978-1-57916-245-0	A Referral Services Business
ISBN 978-1-57916-246-7	A Hair Styling Salon Business
ISBN 978-1-57916-247-4	A Child Care Service Business

How-To Business Books

ISBN	Title
ISBN 978-1-57916-248-1	How to Buy and Sell A Business
ISBN 978-1-57916-249-8	How to Advertise A Small Business
ISBN 978-1-57916-250-4	How to Write A Successful Business Plan
ISBN 978-1-57916-251-1	How to Finance Your Business for the 21st Century
ISBN 978-1-57916-252-8	How to Market Your Business for the 21st Century
ISBN 978-1-57916-152-1	How to Start & Manage Your Own Business
ISBN 978-1-57916-152-1	How to Start & Manage a Home Based Business
ISBN 978-1-57916-152-1	How to Start a Participative Management Program

To Order Business Plans

Please Remit To:
Lewis & Renn Associates
10315 Harmony Drive
Interlochen, Michigan 49643

ISBN # _____ Title _____

ISBN # _____ Title _____

Name _____

Address_____

City _____

State_____ Zip _____

Business Book _____

U.S. Shipping & Postage **$ 3.00**

Total _____